THE EMERGING NATIONS

Their Growth and United States Policy

AUTHORS

Francis M. Bator

Donald L. M. Blackmer

Richard S. Eckaus

Everett E. Hagen

Daniel Lerner

Max F. Millikan

Ithiel de Sola Pool

Lucian W. Pye

Paul N. Rosenstein-Rodan

Walt W. Rostow

A study from the Center for International Studies
Massachusetts Institute of Technology

THE EMERGING NATIONS

Their Growth and United States Policy

Edited by

MAX F. MILLIKAN

and

DONALD L. M. BLACKMER

Boston • Toronto

LITTLE, BROWN AND COMPANY

Published simultaneously in Canada
by Little, Brown & Company (Canada) Limited

PRINTED IN THE UNITED STATES OF AMERICA

FOREWORD

THIS BOOK is in several senses an experiment.

First, it represents an exercise in interdisciplinary analysis. For some years the Center for International Studies has been conducting a series of separate studies in the economics, politics, sociology, and psychology of the underdeveloped parts of the world. We recently concluded that the time had come to try to weave the various insights gained from this research into a reasonably integrated account of the transition through which the emerging nations are passing. What is here offered is not a theory of national development. Rather, it is an attempt by a number of people who have been approaching a problem from different directions and with different interests to explore in a tentative way the relationships among the elements they have been studying. We hope that the outcome will be of interest to those concerned with the problems of development, particularly to students, policy-makers, and the nonprofessional public.

Second, the book is an experiment in collective authorship. Its substance was developed in a working seminar which continued for many months, with the result that every section bears the imprint of an interaction of minds. In the process of drafting and redrafting, the contribution of each author became virtually impossible to identify. Although this procedure has its drawbacks, and we would hardly recommend it as standard practice, it also has real merits. No one of the authors would have ventured to undertake on his own an interdisciplinary analysis of such a complex phenomenon, differing as it does in each developing country. Whether or not others will profit from this pooling of intellectual resources remains to be seen, but there is no doubt that we ourselves have done so. In presenting and defending his own point of view, not always dispassionately, each of us has emerged with a fuller understanding of the transition process and its implications for policy. Inevitably, some of the more personal insights and interpretations have had to be sacrificed in the effort to achieve a working consensus, but the ideas which have not found their way into this book should soon appear in works of individual authorship, perhaps tempered by their passage through the fires of debate.

As with any such collaborative effort, therefore, not every contributor would subscribe to every statement or shade of meaning; indeed, the manuscript in its final form could not be reviewed by all the authors, many of whom were absent from Cambridge during at least part of the period of revision. Although the book reflects a substantial consensus among its contributors, the editors have assumed responsibility for the final selection and formulation of ideas from a rich and apparently inexhaustible supply.

Finally, the book represents an effort to see whether an attempt to enlarge our understanding of the forces at work in the transitional nations can throw light on problems of United States policy. The immediate incentive for the book was a request from the Senate Committee on Foreign Relations for a report on "Economic, Social, and Political Change in the Underdeveloped Countries and Its Implications for United States Policy." A draft of the manuscript was submitted to the Senate in January 1960 in response to that request. This book is an extensive revision of that document. Our concern in the policy sections of the book has not been with the design and operation of American programs so much as with their conceptual framework. Past weaknesses in policy seem to us to have resulted less from administrative or organizational failure than from inadequate attention to the broad purposes and rationale of our relations with the transitional nations.

This book, like most of those produced at the Center, would be less coherent and less literate without the dedicated services of the Center's chief editor, Richard W. Hatch. With her usual great skill and persistence, Mrs. Jean P. S. Clark undertook the proofreading and other responsibilities associated with production of the book. We are indebted to Mr. Granville H. Sewell for research assistance, particularly on problems of analyzing relationships among various aspects of development, and to Mrs. Sewell for compiling an extended list of books and articles on development from which was taken the bibliography at the end of the book. Finally, the authors owe a real debt to the much larger company of scholars who have participated over the last decade in the Center's program of research on the underdeveloped countries.

Max F. Millikan

Donald L. M. Blackmer

Cambridge, Massachusetts
April, 1961

PREFACE

Outside the Communist bloc, more than a billion human beings accustomed to life in the setting of a traditional society are now learning to adapt themselves to the requirements of modern life. Close to another billion people living under a Communist system are going through a special version of this process.

Although the passing of traditional societies seems inevitable, the shape of the new order is not yet clear. In the nations outside the Communist bloc, the results of the transitional process will be deeply affected by what the United States is and what it does. In part, this results simply from the nature of the modern world and of America's position in it. Although the United States represents only about 6 per cent of the world's population, it produces about a third of its goods and wields a major fraction of its military power. American technology penetrates the most remote areas. American political philosophy is studied widely; its culture and values are carried by modern communications into every society. Whether Americans will it or not, their actions influence peoples everywhere.

Moreover, the relationship is reciprocal. The most vital interests of the United States will be affected in critical ways by the manner in which the transition to modern life occurs throughout the world. Our political influence, our military position, our economic health, the entire quality of life in our society will depend in some measure on how the evolution of the traditional societies proceeds. In consequence, therefore, we should be concerned to see that the influence of the United States is exerted to help these societies move in directions compatible both with their long-run interests and with our own.

If the attempts of moderate leaders to modernize by persuasion and consent should consistently be blocked by a repressive ruling oligarchy, those who see the need for change may easily turn to extremist conspiratorial leaders in an effort to overthrow the old regime. Change under such circumstances will be violent and radical, and the society will risk being brought under the domination of an outside power. Moreover, should the West and the United States in particular become identified with reactionary or repressive groups, those who seek healthy change are likely, if they do gain power, to join with forces opposed to the West.

On the other hand, if more moderate leaders succeed in gaining power and in making progress toward meeting the aspirations of major social groups, if they work out means for transferring power democratically from one generation to the next, if they provide constructive outlets for the newly released energies of their people, their societies may evolve into self-confident, independent democracies able to play a full and cooperative role in the world community.

It is in the interest of the United States to see emerging from the transition process nations with certain characteristics. First, they must be able to maintain their independence, especially of powers hostile or potentially hostile to the United States. Second, they must not resort to violence in their relations with other states. Third, they must maintain an effective and orderly government without recourse to totalitarian controls, a condition which in turn requires them to make steady progress toward meeting the aspirations of their people. Fourth, they must accept the principles of an open society whose members are encouraged to exchange ideas, goods, values, and experiences with the rest of the world; this implies as well that their governments must be willing to cooperate in the measures of international economic, political, and social control necessary to the functioning of an interdependent world community. This study suggests some guides for action which will influence the transitional process in the emerging nations so that these interests may be served.

Our concern with world-wide economic, social, and political change is not, however, America's concern alone. It is the concern of every modern society in the free world, for these other nations must also reconcile their international policies with the rising tide of change in the underdeveloped countries. Furthermore, we believe that nothing in the set of American interests enumerated here need be in any way inconsistent with the legitimate interests of the people of any independent nation anywhere in the world, and that these shared interests can be advanced only by mutual understanding and effort.

The first part of this study examines the nature and dynamics of the transition from a traditional to a modern society. It emphasizes the many-sided nature of the process and the wide range of differences that inevitably characterize the modernization experience of societies with different histories, different cultures, different resource endowments, and different geographical positions. It also attempts to isolate certain common features of the transitional process and certain strategic factors which are susceptible to external influence and which will inevitably be affected by what the United States does or fails to do.

History has endowed Americans with little instinctive knowledge of the transitional process. The United States developed in a virtually empty continent mainly from British social and political foundations; and the British who moved to this country in the seventeenth century came from a society which had already gone far along the road to modernization. It is true that parts of their national experience might have helped Americans gain some insight into the process. In particular the slow emergence of the American South from a traditional way of life, with the resulting pain and conflict, might well have drawn attention to the profound resistances of deeply ingrained attitudes and ways of living to the social, economic, and political demands of modern life. On the whole, however, Americans have not been deeply touched by the experience of transition. They have belonged to a society lucky enough to be "born free"; a society that did not have to struggle against the weight of the attitudes, values, and institutions that go with a traditional society. It is important that Americans now begin to grasp what the transition from a traditional to a modern society means for the people experiencing it.

Whatever form the transition takes, it will bring about profound and more rapid changes in the world environment than any which have occurred before. The rate of change in the world has accelerated so greatly that statesmen and their peoples can no longer afford to learn to know their environment through patient trial and error. Unless Americans make an extraordinary and explicit effort to comprehend what is happening to the complex world they live in, they will fail to develop policies with the insight, patience, and lack of illusion required to advance their interests and the cause of freedom.

We present our analysis with some diffidence. The social sciences have developed as specialized and rather narrow disciplines. Some of them have a built-in bias toward static, cross-sectional analysis which ill suits them for use in considering a world scene undergoing rapid change. No social science discipline is yet very skilled in dealing with the complex interaction among political, social, economic, psychological, and cultural elements which the transitional process of its nature involves. We are sure that such a dynamic and interrelated analysis of the transitional process must underlie a sensible and effective American policy toward Asia, the Middle East, Africa, and Latin America; but we are also aware that the analysis offered here is neither final nor definitive. We present it in the conviction that whatever the weaknesses of social science and social scientists, governments must act; and in the belief that they will act better rather than worse if social scientists accept the responsibility of linking their perceptions to the choices that confront governments.

THE AUTHORS

CONTENTS

II. Implications for Policy

The Transitional Process

PART I

The Transitional Process

Chapter One

THE TRADITIONAL SOCIETY

THE NATURE of the transitional process which we are considering here—and which American policy confronts in many parts of the world—takes its start from the character of the traditional societies that are in the process of being superseded. We begin, therefore, by sketching briefly the major features of traditional societies.

These were societies with hereditary hierarchical rule, living under the sway of customs rather than of law. Their economies were static and remained at the same level of limited technology and low income from one generation to the next. Even though some ancient societies exhibited high proficiency in certain directions, they should be termed traditional since they were incapable of generating a regular flow of inventions and innovations and of moving into a phase of sustained economic growth. Before the appearance of the modern scientific attitude and of advances in basic scientific knowledge, no society could produce a continuing flow of new technology. It followed from this limitation that the bulk of men's economic activity was taken up in acquiring food. Typically, at least 75 per cent and often more of the working force in traditional societies was in agriculture.

3

History offers us a wide range of such societies. Some were relatively primitive tribes living within a narrow region, on a self-sufficient base, with tribal rather than territorial political and economic organization, and tenuously connected if at all with other tribes and regions. In parts of Africa and in some areas elsewhere we can still find such isolated and primitive forms of social, political, and economic organization.

Other traditional societies have been made up of loosely organized regions, with fairly elaborate structures of political and social organization and quite sophisticated agricultural techniques, but weak or nonexistent central governments. Medieval Europe, for example, could be described in some such terms, as well as India before the arrival of the European colonial powers.

But some traditional societies were very substantial empires with quite powerful centralized governments, manipulating a corps of civil servants and a military establishment, capable of collecting taxes and maintaining public works over large areas, capable of conquering and administering other regions and of generating a framework for elaborate patterns of trade and even significant industrial development. The Roman and Mayan Empires were such elaborate traditional organizations, as were certain of the Chinese dynasties at the peak of their effectiveness and some of the Middle Eastern empires at various stages of history.

Nor were these societies all primitive intellectually. Some of them, such as the Greek and Chinese, developed philosophy and the arts to levels hardly since surpassed. Societies of the Near East developed the modern alphabet and the number tools on which modern achievements in mathematics are built. In traditional societies of the West there evolved the concept of monotheism, and then Christianity; in India, Buddhism.

The history of traditional societies, and notably of those that had reasonably strong centralized governments, was not static. In times of peace, more acreage was cultivated, trade expanded, the population increased; the government collected taxes efficiently, maintained the irrigation works, and enlarged the opportunities for commerce. The nation extended its boundaries and learned how to administer a large empire. Colonization of distant areas occurred. But then change would come to a halt, and governmental administration would begin to disintegrate; the society would break down. The immediate causes of collapse were various—population pressure, war, disintegration of central rule, and so on. But behind these varied events lay one common circumstance: the society had encountered a new condition to which it could not adapt. Old patterns of behavior persisted even though new circumstances required changed behavior, and the society ceased to function well enough to prevent disaster.

It followed from the preponderant role of agriculture that the ownership and control of land was a decisive factor in social prestige and, usually, in political influence. In some places the bulk of the land was owned by a relatively small number of nobles and the king, and worked by peasants who stood in a feudal, hierarchical relationship to the owners. This condition still exists, for example, in parts of the Middle East. In other countries landownership was quite widely spread, as it was in China, resulting in an endless struggle by the peasants to acquire more land, to establish an economic position relatively independent of the luck of the harvests, and thus to rise in the society. In many of the African tribes, land was owned communally, with no concept of individual tenure and thus little incentive for systematic investment in improvements.

In traditional societies, face-to-face relationships were extremely important, as were the ties to family and clan. Men tended to be bound together and to be valued by one another in terms of such intimate connections rather than because of their ability to perform specific functional tasks. It was very rarely that the average person had dealings with anyone he did not know quite well. Social, political, and even economic relations with strangers were seen as neither necessary nor desirable. Hence human intercourse, which in modern societies would be guided by functional considerations of economic benefit, political advantage, technical exchange, and the like, were in traditional societies much more influenced by codes of friendship, family and tribal loyalty, and hierarchical status.

Although traditional societies sometimes provided a channel for able men of the lower economic classes to rise in power and prestige (often through the civil service and the military establishment), there was a tendency for people to assume that the status of their children and grandchildren would be similar to that of their parents and grandparents. A kind of long-run fatalism pervaded traditional societies despite the ebb and flow of family fortunes and despite the slow evolution of the society as a whole.

The cultural and religious life of traditional societies, and the values they elevated, varied widely. Generally, however, they formed a coherent pattern, giving men a reasonably orderly rationale for the relatively stable round of life they faced, at whatever level in the society they found themselves. They provided a set of relationships of men to one another and to the world about them which gave them a degree of security in facing their appointed destiny within the traditional structure.

Chapter Two

THE DISRUPTION OF
TRADITIONAL SOCIETIES

THE ACCEPTED Western characterization of the traditional societies as static is on the whole an accurate one; and the weight of historical evidence seems to support the view that in general it was the shock and continuing aftereffects of contact with more advanced societies that first cracked and then broke up the traditional social structures of what, for want of a better term, we call the underdeveloped countries. The impact of the more advanced societies of the West has certainly been the most dramatic disruptive influence upon traditional societies. In some instances, indeed, it has been the sole influence, as, for example, throughout tropical Africa, where European nations moved in on extremely primitive traditional societies which had remained essentially unchanged for countless generations. Yet this is not the whole story. It would be wrong to conclude that there were no seeds of change, no potential for modernization, in the traditional societies themselves. There have been significant instances in which the effects of Western intrusion were sharply affected by the nature of changes which had already begun to have their impact on the traditional society. It is worth noting some of them before we turn to the consequences of the Western impact.

Disequilibrium within Traditional Societies

That change in traditional societies is not determined solely by the impact of the West is clear from the comparative history of India, Indonesia, China, and Japan. The English were well established in India and the Dutch in Indonesia by the middle of the sixteenth century, and channels for the introduction of Western skills and ideas were far more readily available than in China or Japan. Next in degree of contact with the West was China, where the powers established trading beachheads at the important ports and carried on trade with the interior of the country. Japan had the least contact of all, for it ejected Westerners during the first half of the seventeenth century, except for a tiny colony of Dutch traders who were suffered to remain at Deshima Bay at the far tip of the main island. What little contact there was with the West was deliberately permitted to flow through the tiny Deshima Bay funnel. Yet of the four countries mentioned, Japan gave increasing evidence of modernization between 1800 and 1850 and was undergoing rapid change by the last quarter of the nineteenth century, almost three quarters of a century before any of the others.

Clearly factors other than contact with the West were at work within some traditional societies to produce men, institutions, and attitudes conducive to change. Some of these factors are highly elusive, such as differences between traditional cultures themselves; some cultures simply appear to have been more amenable to change than others. Accidents of history and of personality have also played their part. Other factors, having to do with the dynamics of social evolution, can be somewhat more tangibly identified.

In some societies, for example, the requirements of conducting war led the central government to enlarge the military caste. The new members often desired changes whose purpose was to increase national power or improve the lot of the classes from which they were drawn—changes opposed by the traditional landowners. This was true, for example, of Prussia before 1793, Japan before 1868, China in the second half of the nineteenth century, and Turkey before 1914. War also increased the requirements for credit and trade, tending to elevate somewhat the status of moneylenders and of those who managed domestic and foreign commerce—men whose formal place in the traditional hierarchy was usually low. In those traditional societies which assumed imperial responsibility, the management of empire itself strengthened the role and status of the civil servant and the technician.

It appears that a traditional society turned the more readily to modernization if there was any articulate group of men in it with reason to be unhappy about their position. Feeling aggrieved, already questioning the values and attitudes of the traditional society, they were psychologically prepared to accept new ways of life as a means of proving their worth and gaining self-satisfaction, status, and prestige. Put another way, the traditional society, despite its surface of coherence and stability, was often marked by inner conflicts; and one of the effects of intrusion from without was often to permit those conflicts to take forms that contributed significantly to modernization.

It may have happened, for example, that after one traditional class gained power at the expense of another a sense of grievance led the displaced class to question the values, the morals, and the way of life of the leading group. In ancient times such social grievances led to armed rebellion, or to migration to a new country, or to a new religious movement, or sometimes to a relapse into apathy if nothing could be done about the trouble. In modern times, if the country has had contact with the West and with advanced technology, and the possibility exists of economic achievement through the adoption of new technology, the restless group may strike off in the new ways of life and lead the nation in economic progress.

A few historical examples may make this process clearer.

In England far more leaders of the world's first industrial revolution came from among the religious nonconformists than from any other single group, even though the nonconformists formed only seven or eight per cent of the population of England. Many other leaders came from the lowland Scots, who had come under the political and social domination of the English.

In Japan disaffected social groups led the way in modernization. In about 1600 one group of clans, the Tokugawa, gained dominance over the entire country and subjected other clans, the "outer clans," to political and social subordination. Under the Tokugawa a national peace was imposed; the warrior class, the Samurai, lost their traditional social position and also steadily declined in wealth. The move toward modernization, which fermented under the surface, led to the overthrow of the Tokugawa in 1868 and thereafter proceeded rapidly, led by Samurai and individuals from the outer clans.

In Colombia the Spanish conquerers inhabited three high valleys which are the sites of the four main present cities of Colombia. In two of these valleys they developed landed estates and became landed gentry or cattlemen. In the third, Antioquia, because the land was less suitable and because other activities were more attractive, they did not. During the eighteenth and nineteenth centuries, as the historical literature of the time shows, the gentry of the other two valleys looked down on the Antioqueños because they too had not become gentry, and the Antioqueños resented this attitude. Today it is the Antioqueños who are spearheading economic and political modernization throughout Colombia.

In India successive waves of migration over several millennia have resulted in the existence of a number of social groups who even today are very conscious of their historical differences from each other. It is probably significant that much of the effective modern business activity to date in India has been initiated by several of the minority social groups—the Parsis, the Marwari, and others.

Thus social tensions may lead to the rejection of traditional attitudes by certain groups, who turn to new activities which may restore their prestige and sense of achievement. Indeed, it is virtually never the social group in control of a traditional society that leads the way to modernization. That group, which finds the traditional social order satisfactory, virtually always resists change, even if the society is threatened from without and change is necessary to resist that threat.

But this social and psychological dynamic need not, by itself, lead disaffected groups to engage in new sorts of economic activities. Modernization must first become a realistic alternative. Only when new ideas and ways of doing things are introduced from more advanced societies will the possibilities of economic change be perceived as real.

The Impact of More Advanced Societies

The initial impact of a comparatively modernized society on a traditional society most commonly took the form of, or was followed by, occupation and the setting up of colonial administrations, actions that had revolutionary effects on the traditional society in two ways.

First, in pursuit of its own interests (and often, too, in response to an impulse to spread the values and advantages of modern civilization) the colonial power executed specific policies which directly affected the economic, social, political, and cultural life of the traditional society. Ports, docks, roads, and, in some places, railroads were built. These were usually designed primarily for the economic or military advantage of the colonial power; but they had wider effects in creating national markets, commercializing agriculture, helping cities to grow, and bringing backward areas into contact with elements of modern life. Forms of central administration and centralized tax systems were usually set up. Some colonials were drawn into the economic and administrative activities necessary to execute the purposes of the colonial power. Some modern goods and services were diffused, altering the conception of the level of life that men could regard as attainable. To at least a few colonials the opportunity for a Western education was opened. Perhaps most important, the colonial power often introduced the traditional society to the Western tradition of law, to some version of those rules and procedures for the dispensation of justice which transcend and limit the powers of the individuals who exercise political authority.

In short, it was of the nature of the colonial experience that at every level of life it brought the traditional society into contact with some degree of modernization.

The character and extent of the contact with modernization

varied with the concept of colonial rule that each power brought to its various colonies. In India, for example, the British made special efforts to train men for both the civil service and the army: the Moslems on the whole opted for military training, the Hindus for the civil service, reflecting in that choice underlying differences in the culture of the two groups in the Indian peninsula. In Burma, on the other hand, the British did relatively little to train either soldiers or civil servants. The French, in their empire, made great efforts to bring a thin top layer of the indigenous leaders as fully as possible into French cultural, intellectual, and political life. The Belgians in the Congo concentrated, for economic reasons, on literacy and vocational training for the lower levels of the labor force and did nothing to prepare an elite for leadership. The Dutch in Indonesia and the Portuguese in East Africa by and large adopted policies designed to limit the extent and the pace of modernization.

But however colonial policy might vary, colonialism nevertheless had one universal direct effect: it disrupted the static traditional societies. In establishing their own control the colonial administrators destroyed the existing power structure. In varying degrees they cast aside the traditional political and administrative system, substituting their own. They often treated the traditional religion with scorn and profaned what had been held holy. They violated many customary and revered human and property rights by introducing Western ideas of law and contract which in the light of traditional morals often must have seemed as wrong to the indigenous people as the Soviet doctrine of the supremacy of the state over the individual seems to the West. In these and other ways the cohesion and integrity of the traditional social and political system were violated.

The second effect of colonialism was indirect but perhaps even more profound than the direct infusion of modern elements. As an increasing number of men in the colonial society became acquainted with the methods and ideas of the West, they reacted against the human and collective humiliation that inevitably accompanied colonial rule; and they sought independence. Some, it is true, were drawn imitatively toward the manners and mores of the colonial power (for example, colonials who were educated abroad or who had positions of privilege within colonial rule); and others found their positions strengthened by the techniques of colonial rule (for example, some of the African tribal chiefs and the Indian princes). But as time passed, a spirit of nationalism emerged, first among educated members of the colonial elite, then spreading to the urban populations, and finally reaching into the countryside.

Colonial rule was not, however, the only form of intrusion that helped unhinge traditional societies. The defeat of the traditional society in war against a more advanced power often played an important role. This was so, for example, in Germany after the Napoleonic occupation; in Russia after the Crimean War; in Japan after its imposed opening to trade by the West in the shadow of modern naval cannon; in Turkey after the First World War; in China after the defeats by the British in the 1840's and by the Japanese in the 1890's. The demonstration that the traditional form of organization was incapable of maintaining the physical integrity of the nation tended to lower the prestige of the traditional rulers, their values, and their institutions, and it tended to strengthen the hand of those groups in the traditional society—soldiers, intellectuals, men of commerce, civil servants, lesser nobility—who for various, often differing reasons were already interested in making the social changes necessary to increase their own power and the strength and prestige of their society.

In sum, the frustration and sense of powerlessness which resulted from intrusion by the West and especially from colonial rule generated an intense, though often submerged, desire for increase in power, prestige, dignity, respect, equality. Sometimes the people seemed almost apathetic about their situation, adopting an attitude which persuaded many observers, including some colonial administrators themselves, that colonial peoples had no emotional depth, no interests beyond the immediate events of their daily lives, no concern about who their rulers were. But when there appeared even a trace of opportunity to express their basic frustrations and realize their desires, the apathy fast began to vanish. Sometimes, as in the Belgian Congo for instance, apathy was shaken off in a burst of violence.

In most colonial areas frustration and resentment came first to a small but important group well before national independence seemed in sight. Some individuals in the colonial society were able to advance themselves by education, seeking to acquire status which both in the traditional society and in the West merited respect. They became doctors, lawyers, scholars. But once they had gained the badge of learning, they found themselves still colonials, still in subordinate political and social positions, still treated as inferiors. Moreover, so many individuals turned to this channel in the hope of gaining the dignity and respect they sought, that some found it difficult to practice the skills they had gained. The result of these circumstances was personal bitterness and frustration.

The continued frustration of the educated colonial has often been attributed solely to the denial of opportunity and adequate scope for the exercise of his newly developed skills. One is frequently reminded of the problem of the "unemployed and underemployed intellectuals," and it is indeed in many countries a real problem. The modernizing societies suffer from a far too large and far too frequent gap between the skills and aspirations fostered by education and the available career opportunities. But other factors have also often been at work. Many of these educated men, for example, attained the badge of university education without achieving great professional skill in any field, which is one reason why they were often still treated as subordinates without high status. In some cases, too, these individuals had become bitter and frustrated long before they received their education. Their interest in careers and professions was not always deep, and frustrations would not automatically have been relieved by excellent career opportunities. In short, despite their relatively high status, some educated men in the modernizing societies tend to remain bitter, suspicious, defensive life-long casualities of the tensions in the colonial society in which they were reared.

The Western example can cause other inner conflicts. After independence, the desire for power and dignity, combined with the recognition of industrialization as a symbol of the power of the West, often provides a powerful emotional stimulus to the desire for industrialization; but it does not inculcate a corresponding desire to live the kinds of lives, perform the kinds of functions, and maintain the kinds of relationships with other individuals that are necessary for industrialization. The fruits of industrialization are urgently desired; the social and psychological changes which go with it may still be unwelcome.

In the countryside, the influence of the West has in several ways stimulated an intense desire by the peasant for land reform. It is not merely that Western egalitarian ideas have led him to feel that he can have something that he has always wanted but thought hopelessly beyond his reach. Rather, in most traditional societies, where population growth was ordinarily extremely slow, there was likely to be no "land problem." Land was not something to be bought and sold. Land often passed from one generation to another of the peasant's family; though the head of the family did not own it, it was his to use, and the lord or chieftain no more felt free to take it from him than he felt able to sell it. Thus he felt secure in the "inherited use ownership" (as anthropologists term the relationship) of his own plot of land. But when Westerners, as in much of Asia, introduced ownership in fee simple, mortgages, and alienability of land, the peasant, after rejoicing in his new ability to obtain money on loan, found that he had lost the right to use his land and that the bottom had dropped out of his world.

Population growth brought land scarcity, it is true, in many traditional societies, a problem that was accentuated when modern medicine reduced death rates so that the traditional level of birth rates, which had previously barely exceeded death rates, brought rapid population increase. In such a situation the peasant would have found himself bereft of land (or without sufficient land) even without the introduction of Western ideas of contract and sale. In such circumstances of land scarcity, as well as when in traditional societies lords used their economic or military power to levy extortionate taxes or to dispossess peasants of inherited use ownership, peasant revolts occurred. They have been a periodic feature of the history of traditional societies. The point to be made here is that, wherever for any reason landlessness or land scarcity has existed, the spread of egalitarian ideas from the West has given the peasant an increased feeling that something could be done about it and has intensified the demand for land reform. From the French Revolution, through the Taiping Rebellion in China and the Russian Revolution, down to the pressure for land reform in contemporary Egypt and Iran, this has been true.

Quite aside from the multiple impacts of colonialism and superior military power, contact with more advanced societies usually led to a spreading awareness of what modernization could do in terms of human welfare. Such contact demonstrated, for example, that public health could be improved, that food output could be increased, and that cheaper textiles could be provided to the peasant and the worker. In the twentieth century the intimacy of communications, including the fact that modern armies have been based in many of the traditional countries, has peculiarly heightened an awareness of the gap between modern and traditional standards of life. Any awareness of this kind, creating as it does a pressure for a rapid increase in popular welfare, undermines faith in the traditional society.

The contrast between the traditional and the modern economy was not solely, or perhaps even most significantly, a contrast in standards of living and levels of consumption. In traditional societies the individual's status and frequently his occupation were determined by inheritance and custom. But once the old society was no longer fully satisfying, he was ready to accept a new image of his social role; and the employment opportunities and the modes of life available in the new cities provided that image. For modern economic activity, whether colonial or indigenous, has inevitably taken people out of their conventional roles and put them in new situations both of work and of life which have greatly broadened their perception of the range of alternative activities in which they might engage. This increased mobility and widened perception of alternatives have markedly weakened the most stabilizing elements in traditional society.

The introduction of Western ideas has also had profound effects on traditional societies. Among the new ideas were the Western notions that all men stood equal before the law, that they should have equal opportunity to develop their talents, and that policies should be determined and political leadership selected on a universal suffrage basis. In addition to encountering democratic concepts, many of the new intellectuals from the old societies have been exposed during their formative years in the West to Marxist and other socialist theories. These have often had a great appeal because they purport to explain the forces at work in societies in the process of modernization. The theory of the class struggle, Lenin's theory of imperialism, and Communist doctrine on the organization of revolutionary movements have gained considerable currency and influence, and have helped generate dissatisfaction with traditional attitudes and values. Although the traditional societies or those early in the modernization process did not necessarily desire to install modern democratic processes, the infusion of new ideas sometimes led to strong movements toward increased popular participation in the political process—a revolutionary violation of the customs of traditional rule.

So much for this backward look at the disruption of traditional societies which has preceded, accompanied, and been caused by the modernization process. Both disruption and the break-up of traditional societies continue, heightened and speeded up in our time by the shrinkage of distances and by the existence of the mass media and the instrumentalities of mass organization.

Chapter Three

RESISTANCE AND CONFLICT
IN THE MODERNIZATION PROCESS

IT IS ONE THING for a traditional society to be moved toward
change by internal factors or to experience the intrusion of modern elements which in favorable circumstances set in motion new
dynamic trends. It is quite a different matter for such a society
to achieve a working modern system which moves toward constructive objectives by increasingly democratic means. Before a
modern society can be achieved—before the modern elements
within a traditional society can become not only dominant but
constructive—a succession of profound changes must take place;
for any established society has deeply rooted characteristics
which yield only reluctantly, with pain and the passage of
time, and only to strong and persistent pressure for change.

Thus time is required for the social structure to be altered,
for new political attitudes and institutions to be created and
consolidated, for the creation of the skills and habits and institutions on which capital formation depends. Above all, time
must pass for new generations to succeed one another, each finding the environment, techniques, and goals of modernization a
bit more familiar and acceptable.

18

Historical experience indicates that no society ever simply abandons its traditional culture. On the contrary, the old culture almost always leaves permanent and significant marks of continuity on the fully modernized society. Nevertheless, the traditional culture must undergo drastic alteration. It is thus of the very nature of the modernizing process that at every step of the way the impulses making for modernization are in active contention with powerful forces tending to retard and to frustrate the transformation of the traditional society into full constructive modernity. There is nothing which decrees that the forces of modernization will win eventual or automatic victory. The interplay between the new hopes and the old ways may yield bloody civil conflict susceptible to exploitation by external powers; there may be efforts to channel the modernization process into disruptive foreign adventures; the society's politics may be seized by dictators who exploit popular frustrations and the inevitable looseness of the transitional period for their own purposes.

In any case, there are three principal areas in which elements of resistance must be overcome if the modernization of a traditional society is to be carried through successfully: politics, economics, and social structure. The underlying requirement for change in these areas is the modernization of attitudes. Modernity is a style of life. The ensemble of behaviors that compose the modern style is given its coherence by a frame of mind —toward the here and hereafter, toward permanence and change, toward oneself and one's fellowmen. We shall undertake to characterize the modern perspective more fully later in this chapter.

Politically, the people must come to accept new forms for the organization of power based on the creation of a minimally effective national government. The balance of social and political power must shift from the village to the city, from the tasks and virtues of agricultural life to those of commerce, industry, and modern administration. The people must begin—in a process with many difficult stages—to judge politics and politicians in terms of policies rather than merely in terms of inherited status or personality; and, if the goal is democracy, they must develop forms for transferring power by registering consent. Much energy and attention must be devoted to overcoming residues of traditional political authority which cannot be harnessed constructively to the purposes of the new national government. Examples are the sects in South Vietnam, the Indian princes, the Chinese war lords, the African tribal leaders. The new government must also develop a core of technically trained men capable of maintaining order, collecting taxes, and organizing the staff work required for the inevitably substantial role of government in the economy and in the educational process. If it is to survive, the new government must also demonstrate effective leadership in establishing programs to promote the new aspirations which modernization tends to instill in the minds of various groups of citizens. Means of communication must be developed between the government and its citizens to convey to them that the national goals being pursued are ones they would sanction.

Political development thus must contend with vested power derived from the traditional society, with a lack of trained men, with a low literacy rate and a lack of other facilities permitting persuasive mass communication, with loyalties limited largely to traditional groups rather than to the nation as a whole, and with the absence of a widespread sense that the new national government is an appropriate vehicle for furthering popular goals. In dealing with these problems many occasions will arise for frustration and backsliding, many ways in which political life may be diverted to sterile or disruptive goals. The Communist appeal to the underdeveloped areas is designed to exploit precisely these possibilities.

Economically, the society must achieve a situation where it regularly saves and productively invests a sufficient volume of its resources, and regularly adopts new ways of doing things. The growth of the national economy must begin to outpace population increase so that continuing economic growth can become a normal condition, a process which in itself involves every dimension of the society and many sectors of the economy.

Resistance to modernization may take the form of certain basic initial economic weaknesses. A very considerable expan-

sion must take place in the number of modern men and institutions, as well as in physical capital, before sustained growth is
possible at rates that substantially outstrip population increase.
To achieve basic economic change, men must cease to regard
the physical world as fixed. They must learn that it is capable of
being understood and manipulated in terms of stable and logical
rules which men can master. Above all, they must desire to use
their energies in manipulating the physical world rather than
regard such an activity as demeaning and distasteful. But such
a change in attitude is not enough. Before a society's economy
can grow regularly at a rate higher than its population increase,
large numbers of men must be trained in specialized techniques;
and these men must learn to apply systematically and progressively to the production of goods and services what modern science and technology have created. The society must come to
desire to use its surplus above minimum consumption not for
high living for a few, nor for war, nor for traditional monu-
ments, but for productive investments. Moreover, the industrial
process itself requires that important nonindustrial sectors be
developed: notably, social overhead capital, agriculture, and
foreign exchange earning sectors.

Socially, men must transform the old culture in ways which
make it compatible with modern activities and institutions. The
face-to-face relations and warm, powerful family ties of a traditional society must give way to more impersonal systems of
evaluation in which men are judged by the way they perform
specialized functions in the society. In their links to the nation,
to their professional colleagues, to their political parties, men
must find partial alternatives for the powerful, long-tested ties
and symbols of the traditional life centered on family, clan, and
region. And new hierarchies based on function must come to
replace those rooted in landownership and tradition.

The small elite groups who dominate the political process in
a traditional society are virtually certain to oppose change, for
change inevitably means reduction in their status. When other
elite groups capture power from them by either peaceful or violent means, the new leaders will be of many minds as to the evolution of their society. Some may seek to divert the national

sentiment and the energies of the new national government into external adventure in hope of redressing old humiliations or exploiting newly perceived opportunities for national aggrandizement. Some may strive primarily to consolidate the power of the new central government as against contending regional authorities. Others may be interested primarily in seeing quickly installed the political and legal forms of modern democracy; and still others—initially usually a minority of the elite—may be anxious to get on with the concrete tasks of economic and technical modernization of the economy.

The confusions and cross purposes which result from this diffusion of objectives inevitably retard the process of modernization. Men may be tempted to seek escape from the frustrations of internal differences and to unite in aggressive attitudes or action toward the outside world. Or they may be led to accept in desperation the unity and discipline that Communist or other totalitarian forms of social organization hold out to them.

Although the small Westernized and literate elites play a disproportionately powerful role in the early stages of the modernization process, the mass of citizens must also be brought gradually into the main stream of change. Each person must begin to assume new functions and new relations to the economic and political process. The magnitude of the change required is suggested by the fact that the transition to modernization usually begins with more than 75 per cent of the population living in the countryside and less than 10 per cent literate. The round of life is tied to the rhythm of the harvests and to the narrow local scene; to a traditional system of land tenure and the assumption that life for the children and grandchildren is likely to be much as it is and has been in living memory. Social life is built around a close family; traditional political and social relations, long sanctioned by custom, tend to be passively accepted. The government is likely to seem a remote and distant entity associated with extraction of taxes and arbitrary recruitment of sons for military service; and the concept of the nation may often hardly exist.

All this must alter if modernization is to succeed. There must be a radical shift in balance to urban life, literacy must increase, agricultural methods must change, and the markets must widen and become increasingly commercial. Land tenure arrangements are likely to require alteration. The idea must spread that the physical environment can be understood and controlled in ways that permit higher standards of welfare. The government must come to be identified with activities and objectives that conform to popular interests. If democracy is eventually to emerge, the citizen must come to accept the responsibilities as well as the power to determine who shall rule and what the direction of public policy shall be.

* * * *

By identifying the three principal areas in which the requirements for modernization may give rise to tensions and resistance, we have in effect defined social evolution in institutional terms. We have implied an approach to understanding the process of change in the underdeveloped countries based on characteristics which are given organized institutional expression in the social, economic, and political realms of life. But the more closely we examine our subject, the more evident it becomes that in the end we are talking not about institutions but people; that no division of the problem into parts permits escape from the fundamental proposition that the paramount requirement for the modernization of any society is that the people themselves must change. Our understanding of the process of modernization in the underdeveloped countries, and in turn our understanding of the policy problems involved, must be informed by awareness of the ferment of individual thoughts and emotions at the core of any drastic change in a society. Here, in what might be called the realm of psychological change, the requirements for modernization give rise to tensions and resistance, to visible and invisible conflicts which are often the hardest for the outside world to comprehend and accept.

To begin with, the instinctive Western feeling that all individuals, or at least all educated individuals, in a traditional society exposed to the impact of modern life should spontaneously value the goals of modernization simply runs counter to the facts of both human nature and history. It is of course true that virtually all individuals everywhere want some of the fruits of modernization—more income for themselves, more power, dignity, respect, and recognition for their countries. But man has ever been ambivalent and irrationally eclectic in his acceptance of the new, and hostile toward innovation when it violates long familiar customs and personal habits of thought. This holds for the member of a traditional society confronted by the demands made on him if he is to reap the benefits of modernization—even if he recognizes those benefits.

Thus to an individual who has absorbed with his mother's milk the attitude that it is wrong to speak or even think freely until the duly honored elders and persons in superior positions have expressed their opinions, the concept of freedom of thought and expression may be an impossible one to accept. He knows that in due time he will become an elder and be entitled to the deference of action, speech, and thought which youth owes to age and experience; and it may be unthinkable that this natural progression to seniority and deference should be abandoned in favor of individual equality of expression. One of the most pervasive carry-over effects of the traditional society is the persistent tendency to inhibit individual initiative, a perpetuation of attitudes that resist innovation in any form.

For centuries in the traditional societies it has been important to the more elevated classes to think of themselves as different by nature from the menial classes. Since one main mark of the menial classes is that they work with their hands and with tools, a man of higher status feels like a menial if he works with or even directs work with tools or machines. It is difficult for him to discard such inherited attitudes even if he is aware of them and tries to overcome them. His distaste for industry is heightened by the fact that the business and commercial groups in such societies (for example, the Chinese in Southeast Asia) are often groups who historically came from other countries and are still looked upon as outsiders.

At the same level of personal conduct, wherever life is economically precarious, as in traditional societies, it is common for all members of a group of relatives to share their income. The individual who gains extra income is obligated to share it with relatives who have less. Should he refuse to open opportunities for financial gain to his relatives because of what we in modern societies would term ethical obligations to his associates or to the public, he may be treated as a moral leper.

Thus the traditional guides to personal conduct become sources of inner conflict and resistance if the individual is to serve his society's needs for modernization. Even the educated man who sees the benefits of modern enterprises is deterred by custom from engaging in them because the practical problems of management are felt to be menial activities. Or, having accepted responsibility for a public enterprise, and understanding the modern criteria of skill and experience, he is still impelled by custom to use his position as a means of benefiting relatives and friends.

In short, the path to modernization opens up an almost limitless range of situations where the individual may be torn by the conflict of purpose in his mind and his emotions, a condition that creates obstacles to every aspect of social change. Such obstacles may be compounded by the high respect for traditional learning which marks many old societies; knowledge of ancient literature and philosophy is expected of every educated man, but study of the material world reflects menial interests and is thus sordid and uninteresting. Reverence for the ancient religion may be a further deterrent to change. One of the authors of this book remembers vividly the fear expressed by the fine old mother of a Burmese boy who had obtained a fellowship to study in the United States—the justifiable fear that in the midst of new experiences in the West he would lose his Buddhist piety. The case could be multiplied thousands, even millions, of times; it symbolizes the underlying loyalty to old values that makes modernization difficult.

The division of heart and purpose tends to be especially great in some ex-colonial societies, where the people as a whole may be diverted from constructive effort by emotions surviving from the past. The colonial administrators, by violating ancient family rights in land and other property, showing contempt for the indigenous religion, and treating the colonial people as an inferior race, may have intensified the ambivalence in the attitude of the indigenous population toward the West. The colonials respected the power of the Westerner and imitated his manner of living, but at the same time they often resented his presence, hated his behavior, and were determined to eject him and what he stood for, including his business enterprises. Now, after gaining their independence, such people may cling to the old all the more compulsively because to abandon it would be to admit that the colonial administration was right, that they were an inferior people.

We must, then, accept the fact that no matter how passionately in one part of their beings men may want to see their societies and themselves enjoy the benefits of modernization, they are capable of sustaining in tolerable psychological order only a limited rate of change; and they may cling more tenaciously than even they are aware to elements in the traditional society as a source of security in a transitional situation where almost everything else about them is changing. Even within the literate elite in the changing societies, who may be quite skilled and may talk the language of modernization with fluency and apparent conviction, there is often latent conflict between the modes of action and the values that modernization requires and the ingrained habits and attachments of the traditional society.

We must approach the problems of the underdeveloped societies with the realization that the modernization process requires fundamental human attitudes to change in such ways as to make the efficient operation of a modern society not only possible but also psychologically congenial. We must be aware that, especially in the first generations of the transition, the commitment of men to the goal of modernization may be more apparent than real.

Chapter Four

SOME FACTORS IN SOCIAL CHANGE

IN THE early period of transition, when a society begins to break out of its traditional structure, the most powerful social class often consists of the men who own or control the land, a group likely to be deeply conservative in every respect. Feeling a deep attachment to the old ways of life, and sensing that social and technological change threatens their hegemony, they tend to resist all efforts to modernize. In Africa, where communal land-holding by the tribe is common, such resistance is often identified less with distinctions of social class than with a widespread commitment to the tribal way of life as a whole.

Where landowners do exist as a substantial and powerful class, their strategy has sometimes been to resist by partially adopting new ways; in such cases they have often retained some of their power as individuals while their power as a class was waning. Where landowners have resisted all efforts at moderniza-tion, the landed class and its members have generally gone down together. The basic shift to urban and industrial life, which is the core process of modernization, has always spelled the end of hegemony by landowners as a class. In tribal societies the transformation is not in the status of a landowning class but in that of tribal prerogatives as a whole.

A traditional society is also characterized by the absence of an indigenous middle class large enough or strong enough to challenge the landowners' power. In the early stages of transition, therefore, the decisive challenge to the landlords' supremacy generally comes not from any one social class but from a coalition, a group that varies considerably in specific composition from one country to another but whose leadership is almost invariably made up of men deeply affected by Western ways of thought and action.

In colonial countries those at the forefront of independence movements have often received a university education in the West, sometimes being trained for one of the professions, such as law or medicine. They may also have been introduced to Western patterns of thought and organization through military corps, administration, and industrial and trade union organizations. In countries without colonial histories, such as Turkey, leadership has sometimes been assumed by military officers whose sense of power combined with a strong sense of national pride created in them a desire to lead the way to modernity.

Whatever their particular background, those who lead the fight for independence, or in noncolonial societies the struggle to displace the landowning class, are likely to be more skilled in the political and military tasks of achieving power than in the arts of governing and modernizing a traditional society. Depending on the circumstances and problems of achieving independence, they may become skilled in communicating with and organizing peasants and workers for disruptive activity, in writing revolutionary tracts and editing revolutionary journals, or in conducting guerrilla warfare. Once independence or power is achieved, they often find it difficult to turn their minds and convert their skills to the tasks of modernization. As a result, the first generation of new leaders is often inadequately prepared by experience and training to deal with the problems confronting them when responsibility is attained. Thus progress toward modernization is inevitably slow in the early transitional period. Groups within the governing elite are likely to contend in an erratic and unstable manner, with frequent shifts of power from one to another. Moreover, the elite groups tend to rally around individuals, the substance of whose programs may be ambiguous and unclear even to themselves. Political activity revolves around issues of power and personality rather than around alternative national policies.

Nevertheless, during this period certain dynamic forces are at work in the society which tend to move the social structure and the political debate into a new phase. First, contacts with more modern societies are likely to increase the number of persons trained in the West or otherwise introduced to modern ideas and skills. Second, the very responsibility of managing a national government, even if conducted without great skill and purpose, tends to enlarge the number of men with modern attitudes and commitments. Third, even if sustained economic growth is unlikely at this early stage, commercial activity is likely to increase, cities to grow, and some experiments in industrialization to be undertaken. Finally, because progress is slow and the high hopes and optimistic slogans that accompanied the arrival of independence (or the proclamation of a modern-style government) remain still largely unfulfilled, there is a dynamic created by the sense of frustration on the part of members of the younger generation of the Westernized elite.

A combination of such forces may bring into being a coalition determined to push forward with a more purposeful program of modernization. The balance of the social elements in such a coalition varies widely according to the initial structure of the traditional society and its experience during transition. In some instances, as in Turkey and Egypt, the coalition has contained a large percentage of men from the military; in others (for example, the Congress Party in India) the military has played no significant role. Almost invariably at some stage in the process, though not necessarily at the beginning, intellectuals and professionally trained men have been influential. Occasionally leaders of commerce and industry have played a prominent role, as did Birla in India. In a few places, particularly in Latin America, individual landowners have also played a constructive part, largely as a consequence of a partial shift in their investments out of agriculture and into the industrial sector of the economy. It is in general true that the social basis for the modernizing coalition has lain in the city and in the essentially urban skills of the elite, particularly the military and intellectual elite, who have adopted Western attitudes.

If this modernizing coalition meets with some success, and modernization actually begins to make a dent upon the society, the pace of social change steps up rapidly. New people begin to take over the shaping of public policy, people with the attitudes and technical skills needed to perform the manifold tasks of urbanization, industrialization, and monetization as well as the complex tasks produced by the rationalization of work and the secularization of beliefs.

In general, and with deference to the variety of specific forms that modernization has taken historically and in the contemporary scene, the central tendency of sociological change appears to be the multiplication of key social roles, in part new roles, in part adaptations of old ones. As life becomes more technically oriented, power and prestige shift away from the few dominant men in the traditional structure—the wealthy pasha, the wise priest, the village elder—toward men equipped to perform more specific functions in the modern division of labor. Professional and technical skills are required for the roles associated with the growth of cities and the spread of industries, the technical advances and monetization of agriculture, the growing dependence of public policy upon an informed and participant citizenry. The banker and the economist tend to replace the landowner and moneylender as sources of cash and managers of credit; the industrialist and manager replace the merchant and trader; the civil servant, the engineer, the agronomist, and others take over special functions that earlier were concentrated in village elders and other men of hereditary wealth or wisdom.

We shall deal particularly with three of the groups often found in the modernizing coalition: first, the military, which is playing a decisive role in many transitional societies today; second, the secular intelligentsia, the manipulators of symbols who shape the slogans and doctrines by which the new ways of life are rationalized and justified; third, the innovating entrepreneurs of many sorts who play a crucial role in modernization.

The Military

With the exception of most parts of Africa, substantial military groups having considerable political and social influence have played a significant role in the modernization process. The likely social origins of the military group in a transitional society, the nature of their profession, and the context in which they operate help explain their potential for leadership.

The top officer group was often traditionally from the land-owning class and committed to the preservation of old privileges and social relationships. But lower officers sometimes came from other classes; their social status was not high, and they were consequently not so firmly committed to defend the old social order. Moreover, because the military has recently had to be expanded in many countries, officers have increasingly tended to come from less elite classes—even from craftsmen or peasant groups—and sometimes are dissatisfied with the old order.

In addition, a contemporary military organization is by nature a modern rather than a traditional structure. In concept at least, men are arrayed according to function and advanced according to skill and reliability in the execution of this function. They are judged by individual performance rather than by their connection with other persons, family group, or clan. While these objective norms have by no means been fully and promptly recognized in all the armies that have emerged in transitional societies, they have nevertheless exercised a powerful modernizing influence.

This influence has been strengthened by the care and resources often devoted by professionals from Western societies to the training of the military, and by traditional pride in military prowess, which has made it easy for restless individuals to find satisfaction in a military career. It is no accident that competent and distinguished military units have emerged in transitional societies well ahead of modern institutions in the civil service, politics, or the economy; for example, the Indian army, the Malay Regiments, the Philippine Scouts, the Arab Legion, the Gurkha Regiments, and the King's Own African

Rifles. As long as these forces were controlled by foreign powers they were naturally conservative—or at least their feelings of rebellion at colonial policies were suppressed. But once independence was achieved, the military could acquire only through the national government the equipment and the professional stature they sought. It is of the nature of the modern military profession to accept a concept like nationalism with all its implications for modernization.

Finally, the members of the officer corps are likely to face an easier set of problems in the transitional period than their civilian counterparts within the new leadership. They may have to undertake military operations either against the colonial power or against residual traditional elements, but where successful, these exercises arouse confidence in their strength. Aside from combat itself, their tasks are to acquire new equipment, to train men in their use, and to maintain with reasonable efficiency the peacetime round of military life—inherently an easier job than to get political, social, and economic programs organized for the society as a whole. Thus it is possible for the army to develop a group of confident officers with modern attitudes and modern skills, operating within a reasonably orderly modern institution administered on relatively modern lines.

Supplementing these broad influences on the officer corps is the fact that those who are recruited into the army are given with their training a certain minimum technical education for modern life. Historically armies in transitional societies have been a vehicle for expanding literacy; and the handling of motor transport, guns, and other military equipment has tended to spread elements of basic training in industrial skills rather quickly through the army. The Burmese army, for example, in addition to the standard engineer corps and signal corps, has special chemical warfare and psychological warfare sections and even an historical and archaeological section. In all the new armies attempts have been made to introduce specialized training schools and advanced techniques of personnel and procurement. Inevitably, then, a certain number of officers and men are being trained in industrial skills more advanced than those common to the civilian economy.

It is by no means foreordained—as the history of the military in Latin America amply demonstrates—that their potentials for modernization will automatically and constructively harness the military to the modernization process. The military leadership may for long periods build and maintain their modern units in a vacuum, drawing important resources from the society but keeping aloof from its civilian problems and making little contribution to their solution. The officer corps may develop a hypernationalism and throw its inevitably substantial political weight toward external adventure, diverting the society from modernizing tasks. It may exploit its unity and high degree of organization to seize power but bring to power little insight and sympathy for the complex civil tasks of modernization. In some instances its political weight has been used to preserve the status of groups rooted in the traditional society who conceived it to be in their interest to forestall the course of modernization. Or, conversely, an officer corps born in revolution may, as in Cuba, seek irresponsibly to keep alive the perpetual excitement of a fighting horde rather than to preserve peace and order.

But history has also demonstrated numerous times, from the Samurai and the Prussian army of the nineteenth century down through Ataturk and Magsaysay, that the military can indeed play a thoroughly constructive part in modernization.

A striking example is the evolution of the Turkish Republic. Although the military played an important role in founding the Republic, Ataturk succeeded in establishing a clear division between civil and military leadership. This distinction was successfully maintained for 35 years despite the continued importance of the military in many aspects of civilian life. The corps of officers who with Ataturk made the revolution and founded its republican institutions were obliged, like Ataturk himself, to resign their commissions when they took up posts of political authority; as a corollary, no officer who remained in uniform was permitted to be active in political life. This tradition survived until 1960, when significant failures in civil leadership and a strong tendency to revert to autocratic rule led the army to take over. The army has, however, thus far shown a restraint in its practices which reflects the impact of the Ataturk tradition. There is good reason to hope that its intervention will be transient and that the democratic process, including the principle of civilian supremacy, will in the end be strengthened.

The Turkish army recruits some 200,000 young civilians into its training program each year. These young men (and women) are often illiterate villagers, whose induction into the army represents their first sustained exposure to men in other parts of Turkey. They are taught to read and write, to handle tools and equipment; they are taught the fundamentals of personal hygiene and public health; they are taught the symbols and institutions of modern political life in a republic. As they complete their training and return to their villages, these young people become a permanent asset in the modernization of Turkey. They put their new knowledge to work; they teach other villagers at home some of what they have themselves learned; they remain "relay points" for information and opinion emanating from the modernized sector of Turkish society. Thus they speed the process of modernization and help to stabilize it.

In summary, then, the military—the one traditional social order likely survive the process of social change—may be able to play a key role in promoting mobility while maintaining stability, in facilitating change while preventing chaos. Upon the efficiency with which the military sector can be made to perform this role may hinge the successful outcome of the transition in many societies.

The Secular Intelligentsia

While the military are strong in their capacity to manage violence, in their commitment to rational institutions based on functional criteria and efficient performance, and in their sense of nationhood as a supreme value, they are often weak in other skills and attitudes needed in a modernizing society. Consider, for example, the basic process of economic growth. Military men are not generally sophisticated economists, and their economic programs are likely to be inspirational rather than productive. In the Middle East, where military take-over has been virtually continuous over the past few decades, instances have multiplied in which new military regimes rapidly foundered on their own well-meant land reform programs. Virtually every new regime has made some more or less serious gesture in the direction of land reform which has won it popular plaudits for a time but which has failed to solve the basic problem of raising agricultural productivity.

Military elites are likely to make dangerous errors in framing and administering laws, instituting and operating schools, devising and sustaining a communication network, unless they are guided by people with professional knowledge and experience in these activities. Such people are the "secular intelligentsia"—the economists and engineers and agronomists, the lawyers and administrators, the doctors and public health officers, the deans and professors, the "communicators" who manage the flow of public news and views that no modernizing polity can do without. They are an "intelligentsia" because it is they who acquire and apply modern knowledge to the manifold tasks of running an urban, industrial, participant society efficiently. They are "secular" because their public roles and social functions are independent of, and usually hostile to, the sacred symbols and institutions of the traditional society.

Often their first problem as they emerge is to win preeminence over the "sacred" intelligentsia, who traditionally performed most of the legal and judicial, teaching and counseling, healing and helping, soothsaying and certifying functions that the secular intelligentsia now seek to perform. In societies moving toward a modern division of labor with increasing urbanization, industrialization, and participation, the new men of knowledge steadily gain strength. But there are continuous frustrations. The doctor is unhappy when people go to the *shaman* for medical therapy, the lawyer when people go to the *shariya* for adjudication, the teacher when people go to the *imam* for learning, the agronomist when people go to their neighbor for weather forecasts, the communicator when people go to the village elder for guidance on moral judgment of public issues.

These frustrations mount as the number of modern specialists expands in an environment that remains highly traditionalized.

The men of the secular intelligentsia become individually impatient and as a group extremist in their views of what must be done. They may form alliances of various sorts—with each other, with foreign agents, even with "deviants" among the traditionalist sectors of landowners and sacred intelligentsia. But ultimately, if they are to make more than a quick splash, the secular intelligentsia ally themselves with the military sector, the bureaucracy, or the business elite.

The historical logic is clear. The other elites have the coercive power and organization needed to maintain stability; the secular intelligentsia have the knowledge needed to effect change. Military, bureaucratic, or business leadership alone usually has foundered because its perspective is too narrow to cope with the variety of problems that arise in modernizing societies; the secular intelligentsia alone usually have failed because their ideas outrun their capacity to develop institutions that are operational. Neither can manage the transition without the other, and so forms the "unholy alliance," which Western social scientists have described (and decried) since Pareto, Mosca, Michels, Lasswell.

The intelligentsia have sometimes been kept from playing a positive part in the process of modernization by becoming isolated and irresponsible critics of their society. Critics they will always be, for discontent is the price of imagination and knowledge. But discontent can also lead to nihilism and fruitless abstentionism. In developing countries it is particularly easy for this to happen. The intellectual knows about the modern world from his reading and study, or sometimes from travel, and he becomes attached to it. He easily becomes a man without roots in his own society. Many college-educated intellectuals do not know a single villager, would rather be unemployed than work in the stink of a mud-hutted rural community, have contempt for the idiocy of tradition. But this contempt is not the fruitful anger of righteous indignation. It is likely to be conflict-ridden guilt and ambivalence. The educated man may see deep inside himself residues of traditional values and attitudes which he is ashamed to admit and which he is afraid to expose to stimulation through participation in the rites of his own traditional culture. Too often the intelligentsia in underdeveloped countries are for all these reasons simultaneously cut off from effective identification with their own people in the villages and from the responsible wielders of power. Such dual irresponsibility may find convenient expression in the shallow platitudes of Fabian socialism or neocommunism, for those doctrines preach modernization while at the same time reassuring their adherents that they are genuine members of the masses and opponents of the newly modernizing elites.

The avoidance of such ideological temptations is not easy. The development of a vigorous intelligentsia is a prerequisite of modernization. Universities, a press, and cultural institutions must be developed, but these are not enough to assure the intelligentsia a responsible attitude. The intelligentsia must be given a constructive image of their potential role. This may be done through the mystique of a democratic development plan. It can be facilitated by programs of international cooperation and intercourse among free intellectuals. It requires also that jobs in adequate numbers be made available for the mobilization of intellectual skills on the problems of development.

The Innovating Entrepreneurs

Entrepreneurs are not necessarily engaged in private enterprise. Among the imaginative promoters of new institutions in the West were many who carried the flag of sovereign authority. There were the buccaneers and explorers on the high seas and in new continents, searching for gold as agents of the king. There were the creators of semi-public exploring and development companies of the sixteenth and seventeenth centuries, such as the British and Dutch East India Companies. There were the builders of canals and railroads. When we talk of entrepreneurs we talk of such men as well as of the imaginative villager who buys a bus for himself to institute a hitherto unknown service, or of the private entrepreneur who raises business capital to build a factory to earn profits for himself. We are not prejudging the forms of entrepreneurship when we say that an aggressive entrepreneurial group, along with a responsible military, an effective bureaucracy, and a secular intelligentsia, is necessary for modernization.

Entrepreneurship is not something that is found in equal portions in all societies. The psychology of innovation has been discussed in the previous chapter. Without an environment that breeds a group of men with strong motivation for personal achievement and habits of hard work and economy, the process of modernization may be long delayed. Entrepreneurs are found in different proportions also among sectors of a single society. In Colombia, for example, the bulk of the entrepreneurs have been found to come from a single valley where wealth could not be fruitfully invested in land. That fact, coupled with certain competitive needs of an otherwise disadvantaged leading strata of the population, produced historically a different pattern of motivations from that found elsewhere in the country. Ethnic minorities have often been the source of entrepreneurial innovators.

The innovating entrepreneur is by no means always in the saddle in a developing country. As a man who is ready to struggle for unconventional goals, he, like the intellectual, is likely to be discontented and to feel himself deprived. As an agent of change and as a man who most often gets his modernizing inspiration from association with alien sources, he is likely to be distrusted. He may find himself fighting regulations and restrictions. Still, the society with which he struggles may be on the road to modernization, despite his strictures and complaints, if it provides him with incentives and freedom to seek ways to reorganize and improve life. The sign of stagnation is not that the entrepreneur must struggle but that no one chooses this role.

The Peasants and Urban Workers

Our analysis thus far has focused on narrow elites—on men who acquire certain Western skills and are in a position to contend for power and to direct the course of events within their nation. We turn now to the evolution of attitudes and skills among the people as a whole and to their slow change from a passive to an active role in the modernization process.

Here again the course of events depends substantially on the kind of traditional structure that existed; on whether the society underwent a period of colonial tutelage and on the kind of colonial policy that was pursued; on the particular setting and impulses that led to the overthrow of the traditional society, colonial rule, or both. Without excessive distortion, however, we can draw a general picture of the changing horizons of the peasant and the urban worker as modernization proceeds.

In the traditional society and in the early stages of transition something like 75 per cent of the population live in rural areas and up to 90 per cent of the population may be illiterate. Mass media, if they exist at all, reach only a small number of people. There are no institutions that permit genuine popular participation in the political process. The peasants are likely to appear apathetic, accepting their traditional lot, but their apathy may well conceal extremely complex feelings. They may harbor, for example, a deep hunger to own their own land or to see their children healthy, educated, and advanced, aspirations that find expression only when a realistic opportunity for change presents itself. On the other hand, as we have previously noted, they may simultaneously feel great reluctance to abandon the familiar way of life, which offers psychic security as well as a protection from some of the crushing burdens of poverty.

In the early period of transition, as urban activity increases, the attractions of the city draw men away from the countryside, even though urban life itself is often impoverished and demands an almost revolutionary shift in social and cultural adjustments. In the cities the unskilled worker is generally left on his own, but in the trades of higher skill, unions are organized at a relatively early stage of the modernization process. Literacy and technical training begin to spread. Thus fairly early in the transitional stage the cities often develop a quite modern way of life, standing as advanced enclaves in a society still predominantly rural and primitive.

The coming to power of the modernizing coalition has direct

effects on both the urban worker and the peasant. Their political role begins to change, for the new leadership feels impelled to make a direct appeal to the mass of citizens. The legitimacy of the new leadership, which has often won out by revolution against the colonial power or the old order, rests in large measure on a real or pretended commitment to advance the interests of the people as a whole and to achieve for all the citizens of the nation the fruits of modernization. At a minimum, the modernizing coalition is likely to take steps to establish means of communication between the government and the people as a whole. This is the stage at which politicians are likely to take to the air waves and to encourage the creation of a popular press. Whatever the substantive accomplishments of the modernizing coalition in its early period of power, and however deep or shallow its commitment to furthering popular interests, its very existence will probably increase the demand for modernization and for an increasing degree of participation in the society's decisions.

This is a point of maximum danger for the developing society. The mass media, bringing news and views of the world to illiterates in their urban slums and remote villages, introduce a new element into the process of modernization. People learn for the first time about the world outside their immediate environs, and their sense of life's possibilities begins to expand. We recall Nasser's statement: "Radio has changed everything. . . . Leaders cannot govern as they once did. We live in a new world."

One danger is that people will learn the fashions of popular participation long before the institutions of representative government are properly functioning. Then pseudo-participation takes command; that is, plebiscites that offer the form of public election without its substance, mob politics-of-the-street in which "popular will" can destroy people and property without constructing better public policy. When exposure to the mass media overstimulates a people to this point, the leadership is pressed to give radio propaganda primacy over political economy. While oratory resounds, development is likely to be shunted to the side and growth impeded. The result, for people led to impose demands which their transitional society cannot yet supply, may be a potentially explosive and spreading sense of frustration.

Whereas the West achieved a participant society as an outcome of the slow growth of physical, social, and psychic mobility over many centuries (the centuries our history textbooks now summarize as Age of Exploration, Renaissance, Reformation and Counter Reformation, Industrial Revolution, Rise of Democracy), the new societies seek to accomplish this sequence in decades. In their desire for rapid progress lies the danger that the effect of mass media will be to increase popular desires and demands faster than they can be satisfied by economic and social growth. Acute imbalances are likely to be built into the growth process by the government's desire to register rapidly those improvements that will be highly visible to the public eye, without due concern for the durability of these improvements. Health, welfare, and educational improvements—often made possible by foreign aid—are particularly prone to prove less durable than planned because the environing institutions needed to sustain them have not been adequately modernized. The common tendency of such improvements is to equip people for longer, healthier, more productive lives. People who live longer multiply every demand put upon a society—for food, clothing, shelter; for work and recreation; for adolescent opportunity and senescent security. People who acquire skills create new demands for opportunities to use them productively. Those who acquire mechanical skills demand machines to operate; those with professional training demand opportunities to practice their professions. If a society fails to supply these opportunities—to satisfy the demands posed by rising expectations—then it must face a "revolution of rising frustrations." In the decade ahead, the strategic question will be how to sustain the high expectations that have already been created in the modernizing world. In some cases, excessive expectations will have to be reduced or revised. In all cases, stable development will require a significant increase in the supply of both visible improvements and durable opportunities.

To analyze such dangers is easier than to prescribe ways of overcoming them. What the new governments must do is to create institutions through which individual citizens can begin to take part in the decisions of the community. Fully as important as plebiscites, representative assemblies, and other instruments of participation on the national scale—indeed probably a vital prerequisite for the successful operation of national institutions—are local organizations of many sorts which can engage people actively in matters of immediate concern to them, and enable them to see realistically the problems as well as the opportunities that modernization brings.

In the villages, community development and other programs for agricultural cooperation and reform; in the towns, trade unions and other organizations; in both town and country, institutions of local government which engage the interest and support of the people—such activities as these help to bridge the gap between government and people, help to introduce content into the forms of democracy which most of the underdeveloped societies have eagerly accepted.

In terms of social change the problems confronting the transitional societies which are led by modernizing coalitions are those posed by the very nature of democracy. Democracy is not adequately summed up in the formula of universal suffrage; the individual requires something more than a vote to guarantee that his interests will be taken into account in the society's decisions. A sound democracy depends heavily on the strength and number of the institutions that stand between the individual and the national government, defending his individual rights in the process of defending institutional interests. While the process of modernization creates some of the preconditions for democracy, its emergence is by no means foreordained. Democracy is a purposeful human achievement, not in any sense an automatic reflex of modernization.

Chapter Five

THE PROCESS OF
ECONOMIC MODERNIZATION

FROM THE VIEWPOINT of the developing society, economic change often appears to be the central feature of modernization. Many of the most evident symbols and symptoms of modernization are economic—the development of industry, the growth of cities, the focus of governmental attention on economic development programs. There are, however, two more fundamental reasons for the central role of economic change in the modernization process.

The first of these is that economic development is a necessary condition for the satisfaction of the host of new aspirations that fill the minds of the members of a modernizing society. Some of these aspirations, the ones most commonly mentioned in the literature, are aspirations for higher levels of personal consumption—for more food, more clothing, more adequate housing. These obviously require substantially increased levels of production for their satisfaction.

But many of the more deeply felt new aspirations relate to aspects of life other than those we usually think of under the heading of consumption goods. These include such things as education for oneself and especially for one's children, improved health, and opportunities to move in a wider circle of acquaintances, to exercise new skills, to achieve new levels of human respect. While these aspirations are not themselves directly economic, their gratification for large numbers of people requires economic resources well beyond the capabilities of most traditional subsistence economies.

A particularly important set of aspirations much neglected by economists are those related more to how one earns one's living than to what one can buy with one's wages. Some of the most significant new alternatives perceived by the members of traditional societies as they come into contact through modern communications with the developed world are those relating to career patterns, kinds of jobs, and new work opportunities not afforded by a peasant society. Again, these aspirations for new patterns of living cannot be satisfied for significant numbers of people without a drastic change in the level and modes of organization of economic activity.

Another reason for the dependence of modernization on economic change is that economic change is one of the key factors causing the changes in values, motivations, and aspirations that we associate with the modernization process. One of the paradoxes of development is that the very innovational spirit which is itself an essential source of economic change is at the same time in part a product and consequence of such change. We do not have to assume narrowly materialist motives to conclude that economic development is a necessary concomitant of modernization.

What then is required for economic development, and how can we describe its essential stages and characteristics? In analyzing the process of economic modernization, we are confronted with the dilemma that the social and psychological and political changes discussed in other chapters are in part preconditions for economic development and in part its consequences. The process of modernization is a seamless web, and the strands that compose it can be analytically separated only with some loss of realism. This chapter is concerned mainly with the economic characteristics of the process, but we shall in the course of it have to make frequent reference to some noneconomic factors.

We can start by underlining the essential economic difference between the developed and the underdeveloped countries. The most significant difference is not to be found in the commonly cited differences in levels of per capita income, or in degrees of industrialization and urbanization, or in the relative state of technology in the two kinds of countries. Although these are all present and important, the essential difference is that in the developed societies continuing growth of output is a regular and normal feature of the economy, whereas the national per capita product of traditional societies fluctuates erratically around a static norm. Once growth has been built in as a regular and inherent feature of an economy, and has been continuing for some time, all the other economically descriptive differences between developed and underdeveloped countries follow as a logical consequence. If an annual increase averaging two or three per cent per capita can be regularly counted upon in a developing country, it does not take many decades to separate by very wide margins levels of living there from those in the under-developed countries. Since there are limits to which expanding output can be used to expand the consumption of the simple necessities of food and clothing, growth inherently involves diversification and some form of industrialization. With growing diversification, the increased complexity of economic interdependence produces urbanization and all that goes with it.

It is remarkable how historically recent is the emergence of societies exhibiting built-in and self-sustaining economic growth over long periods. It is only within the last two centuries that such growth has made its appearance, first in England and then in Western Europe and the United States. It is only in very recent years that economists have begun to study systematically the process of transition from roughly stationary to regularly growing levels of per capita income.

Looking at the gross statistics, one of the authors of this study, W. W. Rostow, has identified in the history of many of the presently developing economies a relatively brief period of from one to three decades during which he believes self-sustaining growth began. He terms this stage of the growth process the "take-off" stage.* There is still difference of opinion among economists and economic historians as to both the empirical and the analytic content of the take-off concept. Some students feel that the available historical materials do not permit us to identify with confidence the period in which growth became self-sustaining. Others doubt that we yet have a sufficiently detailed analytic understanding of the variables interacting in what has been called the take-off to make even conditional predictions as to the circumstances under which it will occur. There is, however, pretty wide agreement that sustained growth is, historically speaking, a recent phenomenon in the developed countries. There is also agreement that fundamental changes in the society and the economy must take place over a considerable period before self-sustaining growth is possible. As we shall see later, the essential characteristic of self-sustaining growth is the mutually reinforcing interaction of a number of sectors of the economy, each of which has been prepared to play its role in the process by a long period of slow evolutionary change. Thus in considering the economics of modernization, and before turning to an examination of how self-sustaining growth is initiated, we must look carefully at the nature of the slow-acting changes which establish its preconditions.

Preconditions for Achieving Cumulative Economic Growth

There is no identifiable historical beginning to the economic development process. In the countries like England which led the development procession, elements of modernization had their beginnings in the Middle Ages. In the presently underdeveloped countries which retained their predominantly traditional, social, and economic forms until much later, establishment of the necessary conditions for growth is proceeding more by a process of adapting resources, techniques, and institutions from the developed world than by indigenous innovation. Indeed, in

---

* For a fuller exposition of his thesis, see W. W. Rostow, *The Stages of Economic Growth*, Cambridge: Cambridge University Press, 1960, Chapters 2-4.

much of the underdeveloped world the problem of how to promote more rapid development by conscious policy is at this point the problem of how to condense into a brief span of time the accomplishment of social, psychological, and economic changes which occurred over many decades and even centuries in the Western world.

We do not have space here for a full exposition of all the features of an underdeveloped society's economy which must be transformed from their traditional status if self-sustaining growth is to become possible. There must, for example, be a reasonably articulated monetary system, an active professional trading community, the core of a modern sector with some manufacturing activity already going forward, a moderately efficient system of government operation and administration with tax and fiscal powers, at least a minimal communication network, and many other elements. There are, however, three requirements we would underline because they indicate the kinds of help most needed from the developed societies in the early stages of preparation for development. They are the expansion of the society's human resources; the laying down of basic transport, communication, irrigation, and power facilities commonly referred to as social overhead; and a radical transformation of the agricultural sector. These three necessary conditions for growth share, for differing reasons, one feature in common: they cannot be established quickly. Each is the result of slow-acting forces which must operate for a considerable period before results can be achieved. This is why they must all have been in process for some time before growth can become self-sustaining.

The expansion of human resources is perhaps the most fundamental, complex, and least understood of these preconditions. It can be viewed both as a psychological problem of generating in enough people the motivations, creativity, and purposeful innovation required for growth and as an economic problem of investing sufficient resources in human capital, of training numbers of people in literacy and in the new technical and administrative skills required to operate a modern economy. The early beginnings of economic growth, as well as the later stages when change proceeds more rapidly, require the imaginative adaptation of advanced methods to the conditions of the traditional technical, economic, social, and political environment. For in no society, even one which has the relative advantage of being able to examine the pattern of previous growth elsewhere, is it possible to take over methods from other societies by simple imitation.

Technology must be adapted to the resource pattern of the underdeveloped country, which frequently differs markedly from that in developed societies. In particular, while in Western Europe and the United States labor is scarce and expensive and capital relatively cheap, most underdeveloped countries have a great surplus of unskilled manpower and a severe shortage of capital, a condition calling for quite different solutions to technological problems. Considerable organizational adaptation is required to operate economic enterprise in a traditional environment lacking many special services available in a complex modern society. Finally, the attitudes of individuals toward association with each other in a business enterprise in a traditional or transitional society are far different from those in any of the industrial societies (which in turn differ somewhat among themselves). Thus it will require a high degree of adaptability for a trader used to dealing atomistically, on an every-man-for-himself basis, to devise new relationships which will enable him to work in a larger business unit. Similarly, it will require high creativity to modify the obligations existing between superior and dependent in a feudal or quasi-feudal system so that a contractual employer-employee relationship will be deemed ethical and feasible.

Our discussion of the forces that disrupt traditional society has suggested why economic innovators tend to appear who turn their energies to the process of technological change, to activities that are in general regarded by their peers as somewhat demeaning. It was suggested that the innovators often come from groups whose traditional status in the society has been lessened and who seek new fields of activity to prove their worth and to gain increased overt marks of status. Thus in England, yeomen, small businessmen, and lowland Scots provided economic innovators out of all proportion to their numbers in the society. All three groups had proud antecedents and history but in the sixteenth and seventeenth centuries were looked down upon by the landed gentry of the Church of England who formed the top elite of the society. In Japan the innovators came in the main from clans that had been subjugated politically for two and a half centuries. Other examples could easily be offered.

While these psychological and sociological dimensions of the changes in human resources required for development are crucial and pervasive, there is also a significant economic dimension. In many of the underdeveloped societies basic literacy is confined to a small fraction of the population. Beyond this, most of the skills on which the efficiency of production in an industrial economy rest are not present. Manual skills can be learned in a relatively short time, but there are also required managerial, organizational, and technical arts which demand longer training and often require years of experience. All such training is costly in resources. We do not yet know enough about the detailed requirements for the investment of capital in human resources in developing countries, but we do know that very substantial investment is needed and that much of that investment requires an unusually long period of gestation before the human product—trained people—becomes available in adequate numbers.

The second key requirement, the build-up of social overhead capital, is more straightforward but also probably more expensive. The dilemma here is that, in the absence of transport facilities, a communication network, and available power, modern industry will not be launched on a significant scale. But before industry has appeared, the visible demand for such public utilities will not be sufficient to encourage adequate investment in the long-lived, heavy, and expensive equipment they need under modern technological conditions. Where, as in England, Western Europe, and the United States, the period of gradual readying for growth stretched over a number of decades, a slow expansion of social overhead facilities was sufficient. In some of the presently underdeveloped countries which have experienced very little investment in such facilities, notably in Africa, capacity must be built in transport, communications, power, and possibly irrigation well ahead of the emergence of a visible demand for them if the momentum of development is not to be retarded.

Three characteristics of social overhead capital investment make it peculiarly necessary to undertake development projects of this sort early in the development process.

In the first place, there are facilities whose products cannot be imported from abroad but must be supplied by indigenous investment. If a country wishes to speed its industrialization, it can import many of the inputs industry needs, such as machinery, steel, some raw materials, and even many technical skills, at least during the relatively long period necessary to develop the physical plant and the operating experience required if it is to produce some of these inputs itself. But internal transport, communications, and power and irrigation cannot be imported; they must be available locally in adequate quantity if the development of all other sectors is not to be held up.

Second, these are all industries in which the most efficient-sized unit is for technical reasons very large. A very small tonnage of rail traffic can be carried only at a high cost per ton mile, power from small plants costs several times as much per kilowatt hour as that from large ones, additional subscribers can be added at decreasing unit costs to the telephone system until it is very big, and so on. For this reason, to achieve the kinds of economies in these services that alone will permit successful operation of many industries, social overhead capital facilities must frequently be built on a scale substantially larger than would appear to be justified by the visible demand at the time of their construction. They are for the most part industries in which the cost of capital per unit of service is very high, even at large volume operation, and this high capital-output ratio is raised still further if demand is limited during the early years of their existence.

Last, most such investments are characterized by very long periods of construction. It takes years to build multi-purpose dams, railway and highway networks, and the like. Accordingly, the decision to provide such facilities must be made well in advance of the time when they will be needed.

For all these reasons, if development is to be accelerated, very substantial investment must be undertaken in social overhead capital during the early period of development. For these same reasons this is a kind of investment that is unlikely to take place on a sufficient scale without active government promotion.

The final economic requirement of the early stage of development which we would emphasize is an increase in the productivity of the agricultural sector. If this does not occur, serious economic difficulties are likely to result as economic change gains momentum. People who are drawn off the land to build roads and canals and factories, and who are moving to growing towns and cities, must be fed. If they were previously productive on the land, their departure reduces agricultural production. If they were not—that is, if in subsistence agriculture the food supply was divided among an unnecessarily large number of workers—then, as some leave the land, the remaining individuals are likely to eat better. Moreover, the population tends to grow faster as economic change gets under way. If food production is not increasing markedly, difficulties of various sorts will result. If the country has been a food exporter, the increased demand for food can easily be met; but diversion of food to meet the demand will reduce exports and thus lower the country's earnings of foreign exchange. This in turn will make it difficult to pay for customary imports, much less the additional machinery, equipment, and materials that in the early stages cannot be produced domestically at any cost and yet are needed if investment and growth are to be maintained. If the country has no food surplus, then the increased demand will require food imports, resulting in a reduction of the foreign exchange available to pay for other imports.

To produce more food at this stage is of course easier where there is a plentiful supply of good underused land—as is true in all but a few of the countries of South America, Africa south of the Sahara, and some areas of Southeast Asia—than in low-income countries where good land is scarce. This kind of difference in resource endowment, sometimes referred to as the "population-resource ratio," importantly influences the level of living in a country. A country with high population density, resulting in a relatively small amount of natural resources per worker, will have a lower level of living than a country with the same level of techniques but with a more favorable natural resource situation. But a distinction must be made between this effect and the ability of the country to progress. If techniques improve, either country may progress; if they do not, neither country is likely to.

Whatever the population-resource ratio, the stimulation of innovation and increased productivity in agriculture is a long and very difficult business. The habits, motivations, knowledge, and techniques of a very large number of people must be changed. The labor force required to operate social overhead capital, commerce, and the beginnings of industry is very small compared to that already engaged in traditional agriculture in an underdeveloped country. In short, the task is no less than to alter, usually quite radically, the outlook, skills, and resources of the majority of the population.

Second, the organizational changes required for agricultural innovation affect some of the most deeply rooted features of traditional society. The establishment of new industries calls for the design of new institutions. This is difficult enough where there is no traditional organization to be overcome. It is far more difficult in agriculture, where patterns of land tenure, credit institutions, legal forms for title, conveyance, and credit, and a host of other institutional arrangements which are built deeply into the fabric of the historical culture must be altered, usually quite radically.

Third, the increase of agricultural productivity in most parts of the world requires the mobilization of substantial additional economic resources as inputs into agricultural production. In many places more water is required; in most places heavy applications of fertilizers are needed; almost everywhere new kinds of seeds, implements, and insecticides are called for. With the exception of water, most of these things could be supplied from outside if need be. The human and institutional changes required, however, if the new resources are to be effectively utilized, are very difficult and very time consuming. Yet they must be very far along if the process of accelerating growth is not to be brought to a halt by shortages of food and fiber.

Again, were several generations available for these changes, as was the case in some of the presently developed societies, they might take place gradually without conscious governmental promotion. Where a country is trying to accelerate its rate of growth, the establishment of the preconditions in agriculture is likely to be one of the most challenging tasks of the national government, calling for very substantial external help both in capital and in technical and organizational assistance.

The Take-Off

The changes we have been describing up to this point will and must proceed some distance before the country is prepared for what P. N. Rosenstein-Rodan has called the "big push" into self-sustaining growth. But a time arrives when agricultural change has been marked and the groundwork laid for further change, when considerable social overhead capital has been built, and when human resources and organizations in many sectors of the economy are increasingly engaged in tasks of economic modernization. The discontent that led to change has become increasingly deep and contagious, so that the pull of the past is dissolving, and the landed elite who dominated the traditional society have not been powerful enough to suppress the unconventional activities that have been emerging or have been too little aware of their significance to suppress them. At this point the tempo of change may quicken, as it quickened in India a few years ago.

For accelerated growth to occur, the preconditions must have been established in enough different sectors of the economy for simultaneous advance to be possible on a number of interacting fronts. Growth in each part of the economy then supports growth in every other part. Many efforts, each of which by itself might well be abortive, so mutually reinforce each other that the economy as a whole rapidly gains momentum.

At this point, precisely because doing a number of things

increases the opportunity to do other things, resources become the critical bottleneck—both resources in general and command over foreign exchange in particular. With substantial external resource help, the economy can increase its output and income more rapidly than otherwise; this permits an increase in saving and investment, which leads to still more output.

If all goes well, the economy "picks up speed" on a broad front. A large variety of previously vicious circles have become potentially "virtuous"; the pervasive interactions between various facets of the economy and the polity which had previously reinforced stagnation tend, as the economy moves steadily forward, to reinforce expansion. More output yields more capital which yields more output. Expansion of economic opportunities aids in the recruitment and development of people with organizational skills who in turn are instrumental in creating further opportunities. Workers learn by practice and then can teach their skills to still other workers. The increased availability of public utility services stimulates demand for these services which permits high-volume, low-cost, low-price operation and hence stimulates still further demand. In men's minds, success breeds confidence which breeds more success; people will be increasingly willing to gamble on long-range expansion and hence will undertake long-range activities which will help promote such expansion. Stimulated by the goal of profit and excellence, and by evidence that improvement is possible, producers start looking for new and better ways of doing things. Technical change in industry and agriculture begins to spread from factory to factory and from farm to farm, increasing productivity, releasing resources for new uses, creating demand for other resources. Ultimately it becomes possible to divert enough domestic resources from consumption to capital formation (in part indirectly, via increased exports of agricultural or mineral products) to assure continued growth without substantial external help beyond the inflow of profit-seeking private funds. Expansion, though perhaps irregular expansion, becomes the norm.

A conspicuous feature of the entrance into cumulative growth is the gathering of momentum in modern industrial activity.

For as economic change brings rising incomes, the rising incomes will create increasing demand for products other than rudimentary food, clothing, and shelter, that is, for industrial products. The industrialization carries the rise in income further.

In the first phase of accelerated industrialization the lead is usually taken by a particular group of sectors. What these industrial sectors prove to be depends on the resources of the country experiencing take-off, on its level of income, and on its possibilities for international trade. Great Britain began with railroads. Sweden began with timber. In recent decades, the development of import-substitution industries has played a large role in the first phase of accelerated industrialization, for example, in Argentina, Mexico, and India. There is no one correct pattern for industrialization. It is not necessary to begin with steel mills. In fact, the processing of agricultural products and raw materials by modern methods can be important during the take-off and during the longer span of the industrialization process as a whole. What is essential is that the society begin to apply efficiently and vigorously modern industrial methods. Later, after entrepreneurs have made their names in industry, some of them may turn their attentions to the land, applying industrial methods to it, so that a second revolution occurs, this time in agriculture. (Some technological progress will of course be occurring in all sectors at all times; what is referred to here is difference in emphasis.)

Essential for the assurance of self-sustaining growth is a sharp rise in the fraction of national income devoted to capital formation. This requires an increased number and variety of institutional devices for tapping potential savings and channeling them into the most productive lines of investment so that their flow keeps pace with the growth, diversity, and geographic spread of activity. During the early period of change much of the private investing is achieved by the plowback of the entrepreneur's profits and by the transfer of savings to investors through personal contacts. This process will not be sufficient for the more rapid entry into growth desired by the presently underdeveloped countries, and active government steps to raise the rate of investment are required. These include restriction of expanding consumption through taxation, direct government employment of resources in kinds of investment the private sector will not undertake, and indirect taxes and other measures to provide private investors with incentives to step up their own capital formation activities. As development proceeds, an increasing share of this function of mobilizing savings for capital formation may be taken over by organized capital markets.

Along with the increasing industrialization and rising per capita incomes will come increasing urbanization, bringing with it changes in breadth of contact, outlook, attitudes, and behavior which have been discussed in previous chapters. Urbanization in the broad sense is one causal element in the broad change in political and social climate that tends to occur under the impact of rapid economic expansion. Successful take-off will reinforce the social, political, and cultural power and prestige of those committed to modernizing the economy relative to others who would either cling to the traditional society or seek other goals. Yet the victory of the modernizers need not lead to the destruction of the traditional groups. Accelerated growth can create opportunities for the traditional elite to find new functions after they have lost their traditional power, and thus can facilitate mutual accommodation, as it did in the case of the Junkers in nascent industrial Germany and in the Japan of the 1880's. Successful economic expansion can act as a social lubricant and facilitate political accommodation and increasing acceptance of requisite economic institutions; barriers of culture and class tend to break down under the impact of social and economic mobility. The very maintenance of momentum tends to persuade the society to persist in concentrating its efforts to extend modern technology and modern organization to the bulk of its economic activities.

The role of government coordination in past periods of accelerated growth has varied widely. There was, of course, no systematic government programming in the modern sense in the British or American take-offs, though there was government participation in some aspects of the process. In Communist China growth is being attempted under conditions of totalitarian centralization.* Brazil and Colombia are contrasting cases. In those countries rapid economic growth began and has continued until recently with very little direct governmental economic activity other than the provision of social overhead capital, and with no central master plan of any sort. Rather, the process has been one of private enterprise channeling its energies wherever the opportunities for innovational achievement and resulting profit seemed the greatest.

In any process of economic development, socialist or capitalist, there must somehow be brought about both a rather high degree of coordination and synchronization of the rapidly increasing number and variety of interdependent activities and at the same time a decentralization of decision-making and initiative to all the newly energized sectors of the population. The coordination must become progressively more elaborate if the process of increasing specialization and division of function (which is central to expansion) is not to result in gross confusion, in plants standing idle for want of essential inputs, in the wrong goods being shipped to the wrong place, in machines falling apart for lack of adequate maintenance, and the like. Some part of this coordinating function can be performed indirectly by the market mechanism. But market imperfection renders it incomplete and slow, and in investment allocation the market mechanism has serious deficiencies. Thus in a contemporary take-off, governmental programming and administration of a number of important processes and relationships are essential.

For one thing, the government must plan its own use of foreign exchange and consider the effects of its regulatory activities on the private use of foreign exchange with an eye to the total needs of the economy. If a government administration spends abroad in reckless disregard of the foreign exchange needs of the developing country—as did the Rojas administration in Colombia—or regulates economic activity without regard to the effects of its regulation on foreign exchange earnings—as Peron did in Argentina—the economy must later suffer the

---

* Rostow places the Russian take-off in the period preceding the Communist revolution, though the subsequent drive to economic maturity has been guided by detailed centralized control.

effects of this disregard. Again, the government must calculate its fiscal policy in the light of prospective saving and investment in the economy as a whole in order that its demands upon the nation's resources, plus the private demands, will not grossly exceed the total availability of resources. Furthermore, there are some types of essential capital equipment—schools, roads, other public utilities—in which private enterprisers cannot be expected to invest because monetary revenues do not result or do not cover costs or because the revenues are so far in the future and the prospect of governmental regulation so great that the project is uninviting. If government does not provide such facilities at a pace consonant with the economy's need for them, economic growth will be retarded.

In a country trying to change its agricultural pattern rapidly from traditional to modern status, both national and local governmental bodies must promote programs of agricultural reform. Even some branches of industry which in a mature economy can be left to private initiatives may have to be promoted by government intervention of one kind or another during the take-off. If the profitability of investment in such industries depends not on a present market which the private investor can appraise but on a market that will emerge only in the future as many other investments are completed and the national take-off is accomplished, private incentives in the early stages may be inadequate. This appeared to be the case with the recent Indian program of steel expansion.

Nevertheless, as even the Soviets appear to have begun to realize, economic expansion will also not occur unless there are growing opportunities to utilize the innovative initiatives of people throughout the society. Indeed, from the point of view of organizational strategy the central problem of a country attempting to accelerate growth is to achieve an effective balance between centralization and decentralization of decisions with regard to the allocation of resources—a balance which will assure that centralization of decisions about the gross scale of complementary activities does not frustrate the creation and operation of particular enterprises on a decentralized basis and the enlisting of private energies to achieve operating efficiency and imaginative innovation.

The role of external capital in the take-off is important. It is not impossible, of course, that a country which is ready to speed up its growth will be able to generate sufficient internal saving and investment virtually on its own. Japan did so. More recently Colombia has entered upon growth with a democratic social structure and with the aid of very little foreign investment. (An increased flow of American investment into Colombia has taken place since World War II, at a time when growth was already well under way and the Colombian market was expanding steadily.) But without the aid of foreign capital, the task will be much more difficult than otherwise, and growth will be delayed, if it occurs at all.

General lack of resources is not the only cause of need for foreign capital. Even if the country's own productive resources were ample, both industrial growth and modernization of agriculture require growing imports of equipment and material that literally cannot be produced domestically; it takes machines to build machines and steel to produce steel. Without aid, underdeveloped countries, except for those few that possess a large endowment of a commodity with an unusually strong and steady export market—oil, for instance—are not likely to be able to pay for the equipment required. Export markets are limited, and in any event diversion of resources to produce more exports would often take longer than the country can afford to wait. Such diversion of resources for exports would, moreover, reduce what is left over for capital formation and hence reduce also the pace of growth. One need not belabor the point: to initiate and sustain growth in the early stages from very low levels of income is difficult without substantial outside sources of foreign exchange even where governments are willing to mobilize national resources to the maximum feasible extent.

As growth proceeds, the new entrepreneurs gain in social esteem and importance. Indeed, growth becomes self-sustaining only if the success of the initial group of entrepreneurs in economic innovation arouses the imitation of other individuals throughout the society, so that the devotion of energies to economic innovation becomes widespread. In economic growth via private enterprise, gradually the entrepreneurs become more important socially until in the country as a whole, or at least in its urban centers, they may become accepted as one of the leading groups.

As this occurs—as the entrepreneurs feel their social power growing and at the same time become impressed by the need for organized national action if economic modernization is to proceed at an optimum pace and by the need for social and political modernization if their country is to be relatively free of tensions internally and respected internationally—they may turn to political life. They may oppose the landed hierarchy that formed the traditional top elite. They will frequently seek the divorce of religion (Catholic, Buddhist, Moslem, or other) from politics, and the removal of the military from political control. They will desire universal education. Economically, of course, they may be "conservative" in the sense that they desire protection of business by the government without regulation of business by the government.

The New Environment for Development

Many of the problems of achieving take-off in the mid-twentieth century are similar to those that countries faced in the past. The early economic tasks still center around social overhead capital and around technological change in agriculture and in the export industries. The necessary social and psychological transformations, too, are in many ways similar to those of the past. But in three critical respects—population pressure, technology, and politics—the current environment is quite unlike that in which the industrialized Western countries entered the stage of rapid growth. In fact, the importance of outside help and the need for a "big push" rather than gradual and piecemeal change are in part consequences of the differences.

Except for countries like the United States and Russia, which had empty lands crying out to be filled, the rate of population increase in the early stages of growth in the past has typically been less than 1.5 per cent and often below 1 per cent. In most though not all underdeveloped areas of the world today population is growing at rates of from 2 to 3 per cent as a result, in part, of the early impact of modern medical techniques on death rates. This does not pose serious difficulties where the countries in question possess substantial reserves of good land. But in many parts of the world reserves of land such as those which the United States, Russia, Canada, and Australia possessed during their periods of rapid growth do not exist. To achieve accelerated growth without such reserves in the face of rapid population growth is likely to require substantially higher rates of investment and a substantially more elaborate organizational effort in agricultural production than has been necessary in the past. It is possible to exaggerate the problem created. After a lag of say fifteen years, population increase creates an enlarged labor force; and, despite the scarcity of resources, this larger labor force can, as cultivation becomes more intensive, produce a large fraction of the increase in food and textiles needed for its sustenance. But with due allowance for this fact, the increased difficulty in economic growth created by an increased rate of population is serious, and in countries where the population is increasing rapidly and economic growth is not getting under way the result may be tragic.

The second major difference has to do with the pool of available technological knowledge. By whatever measure, this is far greater than that available to countries industrializing during the nineteenth and even the early twentieth century. To some degree, of course, other late-comers have enjoyed an advantage of this sort (for example, Germany, Russia, Japan). But there has been a change, in degree if not in kind, even during the past fifty years. On balance, this circumstance favors growth, though it is not an unmitigated blessing. It certainly offers the possibility of accelerating development; there is no waiting for the invention of the steam engine or the automatic loom. But it also complicates the problem of growth. Technological change which has decreased the dependence of some countries on foreign raw material supplies has also reduced the ability of other countries to earn foreign exchange. Technological change which has increased the advantages of large-scale operation has also compounded the problem of organization and capital scarcity. Nowadays, first steps in many branches of industry and in utilities must be giant steps.

A third major change in the environment has to do with political structure and with political and social attitudes. The world is in upheaval today; the peoples of underdeveloped lands have a growing sense of power in their hands, and at the same time a sense of uncertainty and a need for security which are sharply different from their outlook a century ago. Furthermore, modern communications have produced popular aspirations and expectations which are qualitatively different from those of earlier periods.

These modern political and social conditions represent both a potential obstacle to the achievement of economic growth and a potential asset.

They can add to the difficulty because universal suffrage combined with new popular wants and insecurities may often force resources to be diverted to the provision of social security and higher consumption instead of being applied to economic growth. On the other hand, the processes of democracy and modern communications may advance modernization. They can, if properly used, increase somewhat the individual's feeling of his ability to change things; they can promote national unity, which in turn is favorable to economic growth; and they can spread more rapidly than in the past the essential knowledge on which modernization depends.

This constructive potentiality is of peculiar importance in the rural areas, which contain most of the population of underdeveloped countries. There the lesson of experience is that the modernization of village life in all its dimensions is most efficiently done by persuasion rather than by force. The economic as well as the human costs of forced modernization are high, as the experiences of the Soviet Union and Communist China attest. Given a program that goes some way toward meeting the emotional commitments and felt needs of the peasantry, national leaders now have improved means of arousing peasant understanding and cooperation.

The Relationships among Government,
Foreign Aid, and Private Enterprise

It is easy to overlook the fact that historically in every case of economic development the role of government has been great. Even in the United States, state governments built free roads, turnpikes, and canals; national and state governments granted financial aid to private ventures for the construction of turnpikes, canals, and especially railroads. While the construction of public utility systems to provide water, electricity, gas, and telecommunication was left to private enterprise to a greater extent than almost anywhere else in the world, construction of streets, other urban amenities, and above all schools was carried out by local units of government and was immensely important for economic growth. In Western Europe the provision of the social overhead capital so crucially necessary in the growth process was almost entirely a public function.

Thus the large role which governments in the low-income countries are playing today in programs for economic growth is only the moderate intensification, not the reversal, of a historic trend. There are several reasons why the role of government has increased, particularly during the early stages of development.

One is that a society close to the traditional stage is unlikely to contain a large number of men with the attitudes toward manual-technical work and its management, toward business activity in general, and toward society as a whole which are required for modern industrial entrepreneurship. To the extent that flourishing private enterprise exists outside of agriculture, it is likely to be concentrated in commercial and speculative activity. Private enterprise in agriculture, in turn, is likely to be associated with traditional rather than modern methods and organization. Hence little creative private business enterprise exists. The pressure to develop the economy soon and rapidly is such that governments feel compelled to step in and act in lieu of private action rather than wait for private initiative to develop.

It should be stressed, however, that the need for trained and creative men exists whether economic development is carried on largely by private individuals or predominantly under comprehensive governmental control. The establishment of an enterprise by governmental order and the appointment of a governmental official to direct it do not in the least reduce the need for creative adaptation and mobilization of new skills. The new government enterprise may not succeed; if the attitudes, skills, and values necessary for creative entrepreneurship are absent among potential private entrepreneurs, they are likely to be absent also among the individuals who are appointed to the management of public enterprise. Yet the governments have no alternative but to go ahead, and in some societies, especially the ex-colonial ones, the public service motivation associated with government enterprise may attract effective managerial talent which would not otherwise have applied itself to commercial or industrial activity.

Second, there are limits to the effectiveness of private market institutions, especially where development must be accelerated. It may be necessary to plan out in advance the key pieces of a general development program. Further, the profitability of social overhead capital does not fully reflect the net social benefits it may provide. For example, a power plant may justify its cost by the stimulus it gives to the establishment of many power-using enterprises even though the power plant itself is not at first profitable; a road or railroad may have similar indirect benefits, and in addition may contribute to national unity and to the development of new contacts and new outlooks on life, which in themselves stimulate further development. The greater the concern for speed in development, the weightier the importance of indirect, widely diffused benefits.

The third reason for the increased role of government during the early stages of development has to do with foreign private enterprise. Foreign activity could help make up the shortage of indigenous managers and entrepreneurs. Why, then, is it so often discouraged by the underdeveloped countries themselves? In good part, no doubt, because of the acute reactive nationalism which often colors the political process of a transitional society.

Foreign private enterprise is a convenient symbol of the external domination from which such a society seeks to liberate itself. Thus, especially immediately following the achievement of independence, the new governments are likely to be unfriendly to foreign private investment and to behave in ways that inhibit foreign capital from assuming what they see as serious political risks on top of the very real economic ones which are in any case present.

A final and most important reason for governmental formulation of a development program in new states is that such a program can greatly assist the political leaders in focusing the attention of citizens on constructive national goals and objectives. Many of the new states are faced with the grave problem of shifting the focus of the loyalties and allegiance of their people from local, family, or tribal matters to national concerns. Economic development requires sacrifice and devotion from all sectors of the population, and a development program provides a symbol of national purpose around which new loyalties can be joined.

Thus the substantial role that the governments of the underdeveloped countries are playing in economic matters is in most cases the result not so much of the ideological preferences of their leaders as of the practical necessities of their situation. Similar considerations dictate that the governments of the more highly developed countries must to an increasing degree take on the function of supplying capital for development which formerly was carried out largely by private enterprise.

During the nineteenth century and up until World War I, a considerable flow of private capital to low-income countries occurred, not only as direct investment in business enterprises but also for the purchase of government bonds. Now that the role of governments has expanded, the opportunities for productive use of external capital by governments is correspondingly increased. But the disruption of international capital markets by two world wars, the great depression of the 1930's, and the structural changes which were occurring have been such that resumption of private lending to the governments of low-income countries on any appreciable scale is hardly conceivable. Consequently, the need for transfers of capital by governments and international governmental organizations arises from fundamental changes in the underlying objective situation.

As development proceeds, the potential role of private enterprise increases. As a new generation emerges concerned less with symbols and more with the pragmatic problems of growth, individuals in increasing numbers are likely to shift their attention to economic activity, and away from the political and military activities which were central to the earlier phases of modernization. The initial inclination of government and of the electorate to limit the role of private enterprise on ideological grounds is imbedded in emotions of the colonial period, in the conviction that the private enterprises of the colonial power were exploiting the country for their selfish ends. Concern about private enterprise continues long after independence, partly from lack of confidence in the ability to cope effectively with private power if it is allowed to intrude. But, as nationalist governments become more secure in their achievement and in their position in the world, they come to realize increasingly that all available reserves of energy, public and private, must be tapped, and that the roles of government and private enterprise are complementary. Even foreign enterprise ceases to appear exclusively as a threat and symbol of foreign domination and begins to be regarded as a limited tool to accelerate growth.

The rise of private capitalism is no more inevitable than the triumph of democratic politics. What is important to emphasize is that abstract arguments on the level of slogans, whether socialist or laissez faire, are almost irrelevant to the real choices confronting the underdeveloped countries. Their problem is to devise a blend of institutions and procedures that, while generally consistent with their ideological inclinations regarding equality, opportunity, and the like, will meet their requirements for growth without resort to totalitarian techniques. In doing so, if democratic institutions have emerged, they tend first to tolerate and then later to welcome private enterprise.

With respect to domestic private enterprise, this tendency is interestingly illustrated even within the brief span of India's development program to date. As recently as the mid-1950's, denunciations of private enterprise by Indian officials were bitter; and just as bitter were the protests by private enterprisers that government regulations and encroachments were making effective operation of private enterprise impossible. But by 1959 the contending parties had come to an understanding; government officials felt that private enterprise could make a major contribution to growth; private enterprisers felt that the sphere available to them was reasonably clear and reasonably secure from government encroachment. Indeed, in the Second Five Year Plan the flow of private investment was so much greater than had been anticipated that this fact in itself necessitated major revision of the program before its end.

The longer-run change in attitude toward foreign investment, as the nation gains self-confidence and loses its sense of frustration and of indefinite evil forces threatening it, is illustrated by the change of atmosphere in Mexico. As recently as the mid-1930's, Mexico nationalized foreign oil companies, and the flow of foreign investment into Mexico came to a virtual halt, paralyzed by the uncertainty concerning future government action and by the general atmosphere of hostility. But after two decades of successful economic growth, Mexico is no longer afraid that foreign investment will threaten its sovereignty, and foreign investment is playing a significant (though subordinate) role in Mexico's continuing advance. Turkey provides a similar example of a reversal in attitude.

The moral is that even where the role of the government in the economy is increasing, the trend will not inevitably continue. The histories of modern Turkey, Mexico, and India are better guides to the future than Hayek's *Road to Serfdom*.

Chapter Six

PATTERNS AND PROBLEMS
OF POLITICAL DEVELOPMENT

IN SURVEYING the social, psychological, and economic aspects of
the modernization process, we have isolated the major forces
that shape and color the realm of politics in transitional societies.
These numerous explosive, but also strangely inhibiting, forces
can so undermine the basis for collective social action as to make
it appear that such countries lack a polity. Political incoherence
and instability are often matched in the sphere of public administration by ineffectualness in action and paralysis in decision.
Above all else, the conflicting processes of change compound
uncertainty, and thus rob the people of that shared sense of the
domain of reasonable expectations which is the first prerequisite
of representative government. The possible and the plausible,
the likely and the impossible are so readily confused in transitional societies that both elation and resignation are repeatedly
hitched to faulty predictions. Thus, in the political realm,
where conscious choice and rational strategies should vie in promoting alternative human values, it becomes difficult to discern
what choices are possible and what values are the truly held
ones of the people. The drift is away from realism and toward

either crudely emotional appeals or toward gentle ideals that offer respectability in Western circles but are irrelevant to the domestic scene.

Political instability comes not alone from the uncertain and jarring changes in the social and economic underpinnings of the political sphere. The people themselves, out of a turmoil of change that is more drastic and more constant than that which is normal between generations, reflect an extraordinary diversity in their understanding and appreciation of political action. The lack of a common elementary orientation to the goals and the means of political action reduces the effectiveness of all. There are some people who still adhere to traditional views and conceive of politics as primarily providing opportunities for realizing status, prestige, and honor. Such views are sustained by constant demonstrations that the masses in transitional societies still derive a sense of well-being from identifying with the grandeur and glory of their national leaders. Other people, taking their cues from the colonial period, equate government with the security of office and the dignity of clerks in the civil service. For them government is above all the ritualization of routine, where the propriety of procedure takes precedence over all other considerations.

Still others in transitional societies first came to an appreciation of politics out of the excitement of independence movements. They continue to expect politics to be the drama of group emotions and to despise those who would give in to the humdrum calculation of relative costs and risks. For such men, affected by what might be termed the "resistance movement" psychology, the politician should be a free and unfettered soul who can remain above tedious consideration of public policies. There are also those in transitional societies who look to politics and government to change their society and who feel that their dreams of a new world are shared by all. Some of these so grossly underestimate what must be done before the fruits of modernization can be realized that their ambitions incite little sustained effort, and they are quick to declare themselves frustrated. Others who accept the need to deal with the prerequisites of development first may learn that all their energies can be absorbed in distasteful enterprises without visibly advancing the ends they seek.

This diversity in orientations, which is dramatized above all by the gap in outlook between the modernized, urban-centered leaders and the tradition-bound, village-based peasants, makes it extremely difficult to identify the real social interests which are hidden within the society. The basic function of representative politics, which is to aggregate the diverse values of a people and translate them into public policies that can be meaningfully administered by governmental authority, cannot be readily realized in transitional societies. Since these societies are not populated by stable groups with stable and specific interests, the processes by which power is accumulated and directed tend to be less responsive to social needs and more responsive to personal, individual needs. The personality of the leader tends to bulk exceedingly large; and even the idiosyncrasies of his followers may be more crucial in shaping developments than the functional needs of social and economic groupings throughout the society.

There is, of course, a psychological dimension to politics in all societies; but in transitional countries, the political process often has to bear to an inordinate degree the stresses and strains of people responding to personal needs and seeking solutions to their intensely private problems. People who are caught up in all the uncertainties of social change may turn to political action in order to gain some element of personal and individual security, to build up links with other human beings, and to find some sense of personal identity. Such people are not to be satisfied by the realization of any particular goals of public policy; for them the meaning of politics is to be found in the drama of participation, the excitement of controversy, the security of association, and above all the reassurance of being superior to and one up on others. For such people, one alternative of public policy can be quite as satisfying as another.

Here both the source and the consequence of instability meet and produce a vicious spiral. Although transitional societies have the greatest need for the rational application of administrative programs, their administrative policies often are far removed from the psychic needs of the people. The need to utilize the mechanisms of politics for solving private personal problems compromises the extent to which politics can solve general social problems. Yet until these community problems are resolved and the society modernized, there will be a continuing demand to use politics for its therapeutic powers.

More fundamentally, in transitional societies the processes of change create profound insecurities in the people which cause them to feel a deep need to be bound to others, to avoid any sense of isolation. These psychological needs tend in turn to cause political leaders—whether they are still conservatives holding to the old values or modernizers anxious for rapid development—to delude themselves into believing that their particular political opinions and judgments must be those of the vast majority of their peoples. This in turn tends to create a compelling need for conformity at precisely the moment when even the rudiments of consensus are missing. Prisoners of their own illusions of consensus, leaders and governments easily believe they represent the true genius of their people. But since they lack reliable measures of popular sentiments, self-doubts still linger on, and leaders may gradually but steadily gravitate toward authoritarian means.

Some Characteristics of Transitional Political Processes

Inevitably the political process in transitional societies must reflect the basic bifurcated nature of such societies, with their division between those who are modernized, better acculturated, more Westernized, more urbanized, and those who still cling to the traditional patterns and live within the rural and peasant communities. Governments tend to be dominated by a peculiarly distinct social, economic, and educational group whose outlook on life is quite different from that of the masses of the people. In all societies, there are, of course, differences in the social perceptions of leaders and followers, between those who are close to power and those who live close to the land. In transitional societies, however, the gap is particularly large because the intermediary position is not filled by individuals and groups who might perform a linkage function by transmitting and translating the views of elite and mass to each other.

Specifically, most transitional societies lack explicitly developed interest group structures. Interests are not represented by groups that have limited but clearly defined demands to make on the political process. Thus, on the one side, the politicians are not informed of the negotiable interests that may exist within the society, while on the other side, the people do not have manifest groups to which they can turn to seek support for their specific and limited interests.

The absence of such interest groups means that politicians lack the essential indicators which they need to make rational calculations of how interests might best be aggregated in order to achieve those policy mixes that would meet the real interests of the greatest number of people. Politicians cannot perform the basic art of the democratic leader of seeking to combine the concrete but limited interests of various groups within the community and to formulate widely accepted public policies which are consistent with the requirements of public order and the continuity of the state. Instead, politicians in transitional societies must address themselves to an apparently undifferentiated audience. They must cast their appeals to all groups, at all times on all issues, and in approximately the same form.

These conditions encourage diffuse ideological and emotional discourse. Unable to match specific appeals to particular groups, the politicians must rely upon gross and unrefined approaches. The same techniques must be employed in mobilizing public support regardless of whether the object sought is petty or grand. The consequence is an extremism in language which seems out of line with the content of policy. The situation clearly favors the charismatic leader, the leader whose personal charm and personality are his stock in trade.

Those groups that do exist within transitional societies generally represent total ways of life; they are most frequently communal groups based on language, ethnic, religious, or regional considerations. Or they tend to represent intensely personal associations and loyalties. Indeed, even the political parties in transitional societies tend to be either mass social movements representing total ways of life, such as the Congress Party of India, or the highly personalized following of a single individual, as in some of the new African states. Thus the two extreme forms of the mass movement and the clique tend to become the key units of political action.

Faced with such circumstances, political leadership must often place an especially high premium upon personal loyalty. The allegiance of followers does not usually depend upon policy objectives or programs, for the people identify with the group, not with its momentary policies. Consequently, leaders in transitional societies usually have great freedom of choice in matters of tactics and strategy. This freedom, however, is more apparent than real, for the leaders, as we have noted, generally lack realistic guides for making policy decisions and easily become the captives of their own imaginations. Those who are personally champions of modernization may feel at one moment that all their people share their enthusiasm, while at the next moment they may feel that they stand alone; and thus elation and despair come to play inordinate parts in the actions of governments.

In their search for guidance, leaders in transitional countries tend to two extremes: they become dependent either upon abstract ideological theories for public policy, or upon the advice of personal associates and friends. Either source can reassure them that they are doing the right thing under the existing conditions, but neither source can give them realistic information about the interests of their people.

The insensitivity of transitional political processes to the articulation of specific interests also means that large numbers of people tend to feel that they are disenfranchised and are without ready access to political influence. The channels for admission to the political arena usually are more related to social and educational considerations than to the intensity of needs and interests. With little warning, inarticulate pressures can build up and explode upon the political scene. However, even powerfully felt needs can quickly dissipate their intensity and have few lasting consequences, for they lack organized form and thus lack staying power. They can become disturbing memories which haunt the political process. The urban mob and the peasant revolt may thus lay siege to the political process, but rarely are they able to influence it in such a way as to resolve the basic tensions that may have caused their initial emergence.

* * * *

Political development in transitional societies involves two major spheres of social organization. First, there is the need to create governmental structures and administrative organizations to handle public policy problems. Second, there is the need to create stable but sensitive political mechanisms for relating the interests and the demands of the society to political power. These two aspects of political development involve quite different types of skills and different organizational forms. The first involves primarily the training of administrators and the establishment of effective bureaucratic structures, while the second is related to the role of the popular politician and the creation of party and interest group systems.

In most newly independent countries the emphasis during the colonial period was entirely upon the creation of the administrative framework of government. Only at a later stage under colonial rule was there any emergence of popular agitational politics and the development of a political party system. After independence, there of course remains an urgent and growing need for trained administrators and technicians to maintain the administrative framework which was created in the colonial days. The drama of post-independence politics, on the other hand, is likely to be dominated by those who are primarily concerned with the second aspect of political development. Unfortunately, the uneven pattern of development in most transitional societies has meant that those primarily concerned with administrative development and those involved in popular political development have emerged at different times and often find it difficult to work effectively together.

The ultimate goal in realizing a modern state and a modern society in these countries is the achievement of a balanced form of development in which an effective administrative structure can respond readily to the demands placed on it by the political process, and the political process in turn can effectively transmit the interests of the people and formulate policies that are consistent with the capabilities of the administrative system. When the development of either system gets much out of line with the other one, tensions are certain to follow. An exaggerated building-up of the administrative arms of government can produce a situation analogous to colonial rule, in which the people feel that they are being dominated by the authoritative aspects of government. On the other hand, when the administrative system lags behind the political one, the people can lose faith in rational government because of the ineffectualness and incompetence of the administrative service.

The most disturbing situation occurs when these two aspects of political development become confused and are guided by inappropriate standards. Thus the administrative system may take on values and attitudes appropriate only to the political system, and in becoming thus politicized it becomes inefficient. Conversely, the political system may turn to an administrative form of politics and depend upon authoritative techniques of rule. The democratic ideal calls for these two aspects of political development to be separated but appropriately coordinated. It is not often appreciated in transitional countries that administrative incompetence and inefficiency are as undemocratic as an administratively dictatorial party system. Whenever political parties and administrative services seek to emulate each other or to usurp each other's functions, there cannot be a stable development of the democratic system.

National Unity and Political Consensus

From these general observations it becomes apparent that the task of nation building in transitional societies is peculiarly complex and difficult. Sentiments of nationalism have been a dominant force in much of the non-Western world, but they have not automatically guaranteed the real degree of national unity essential to the functioning of a modern nation state. Although creation of genuinely sovereign political entities in a transitional world requires the building of both more effective administrative structures and more sensitive political processes, the first pre-requisite is a sense of national unity, a political consensus. The form of national unity which an administrative system can give to a people is not enough, for new countries must also be able to cope with diversity at the political level.

In many countries the problem of national unity and political consensus takes the form of an elementary question of what should be the physical and psychological definitions of the national identity. Some new states—Pakistan and Indonesia are notable examples—are split into widely separated parts, and even those which are physically in one piece usually suffer from poorly developed communication and transportation systems, making it difficult for them to perform as integrated national units. Most of the new countries, moreover, are uncertain about the extent of their territory. Their boundaries often follow the arbitrary administrative divisions imposed by European colonial powers in Africa, the Middle East, and southern Asia, which tended to ignore tribal and cultural differences. Especially in Africa, conflicts seem inevitable as peoples and their new govern-ments assert "legitimate" claims to territory that finds itself under another flag.

Disruptive as are the problems of physical unification, they are perhaps more susceptible to solution than a deeper set of problems involving the attitudes and loyalties of people within a given state. The spirit of nationalism and the struggle for independence create in many of the new countries an illusory sense of national unity. Once independence is achieved, how-ever, the old ethnic, linguistic, religious, or tribal loyalties tend to reassert themselves with renewed strength: India had to be divided into two countries, Burma has had to fight five separatist movements, Indonesia has been torn by the divisive forces of fanatical Muslims and non-Javanese nationalists, Ghana has had the opposition of the Ashanti chiefs, and more casualties have resulted from intertribal fighting in the Congo than from the attacks on Europeans.

Such communal divisions have resulted particularly wherever the new national leadership has been recruited largely from a single region or ethnic group, or where it is a conspicuously Westernized elite trying to impose alien values on the society. Tensions appear in most dramatic and dangerous form where there exist large racial minorities performing key economic roles; in Southeast Asia there are the Chinese and Indian populations; in Africa, the Asians and above all the white settlers. In many transitional societies the multiracial problem dominates politics; until it is resolved little progress is likely to be made.

Some of the societies of mixed race contain enclaves of highly modern economic and social activities, as in the Central African Federation for example, where substantial numbers of Europeans live and work at levels of welfare and technology roughly equivalent to those in Europe, while the bulk of the native population remains close to traditional life. Enclaves of a less dramatic character exist in certain societies endowed with rich natural resources such as oil and minerals which have been exploited, mainly for export, by a small number of Europeans. These enclaves of modern economic activity have not usually stimulated modernization in the society as a whole; and they have often tended to aggravate existing racial, social, economic, and nationalist conflicts. Such highly visible enclaves are but intensified versions of a fairly general condition. It is typical of modernizing societies that certain geographic regions acquire advanced technology earlier than others, and that modern ways spread out only gradually to the rural areas. India and Brazil, for example, also contain large areas still close to the pattern of traditional life. The divisions in basic outlook which are associated with such a cleavage make national unity a difficult goal to attain. There may be extremely few commonly shared values in a society composed of highly Westernized intellectuals and technicians at the one extreme and of peasants or tribal members at the other. Indeed, the barriers between different linguistic groups are usually more easily bridged than those which separate the modernized from the more traditional people. Such barriers frustrate the development of a workable political consensus.

In sum, the issues of national unity represent basic constitutional problems. Only as they are resolved can a society develop its policy and create the means for grappling with the social and economic problems of modernization.

Patterns of Political Development

The political development of the transitional societies is clearly a critical factor shaping the world environment in which our own nation must function. The American national interest will be directly affected by the courses taken by the transitional societies as they move to create national unity. Some may lead in promising directions, others may pose a threat to our national security. In this context certain general considerations apply to the over-all process of political development in the newly emergent countries.

Our biggest problems are likely to stem from weak and divided societies. Our goal should be to encourage the growth of states that are strong and effective but in which power comes to be increasingly widely shared among groups throughout the society. Dictatorships can be strong and effective in the short run—and may indeed be a necessary stage through which some of the transitional societies will have to pass—but they provide no permanent solution to the problem of national unity in the underdeveloped countries. Governments that cannot muster the support of the major groups in a society and begin to satisfy their physical and psychological needs by setting them to work on constructive tasks will in the long run be insecure and liable to violent overthrow. The heart of the problem of achieving national unity is that the people themselves, not merely their governments, must acquire a sense of responsibility for and sharing in the process of political as well as social modernization.

It is in the light of these broad considerations that we now consider some of the possible patterns and courses of political development in the new countries as they confront the problems of change and the task of creating national unity. There is obviously neither a single inevitable course which all countries will follow nor any set of political conditions applying identically to any two countries. Nevertheless, it does seem possible to divide the transitional societies into meaningful groupings according to their common problems and political characteristics and to suggest some common patterns of political development that may apply to each group. We have found it useful in thinking about the problems of political development to classify the transitional countries into three groups: neo-traditional oligarchies, transitional oligarchies, and actively modernizing democracies. Like any classification this one is arbitrary in many respects, but it may help to illustrate certain central differences in existing political systems and to focus attention on their potentialities for evolution.

Neo-Traditional Oligarchies

These are nations which have already felt the impact of the modernized world and have incorporated certain modern elements into their life but have not developed very far beyond their traditional forms. Most of these countries are monarchies based upon an authoritarian structure of society, and the degree of their national unity may be relatively high as compared to that of countries more deeply affected by the modern world. The national leaders may feel it necessary to incorporate some modern elements into their political forms, and they may even accept democratic symbols; but the test of participation in politics generally hinges upon questions of loyalty and allegiance rather than upon capability to perform modern tasks. Typical examples of such countries are Ethiopia, Saudi Arabia, Jordan, Yemen, and Iran in the Middle East and Africa, and Cambodia and Laos in Asia.

The obstacles to developing more modernized structures of authority to replace the traditional ones are reflected in the basic indexes of development for these societies. The average literacy rate of the Asian and African societies we would classify as neo-traditional oligarchies is slightly less than 10 per cent of the population; and in three-fourths of these countries the rate is somewhat under 5 per cent. The annual per capita gross national product is less than $100 in all but two countries for which oil production gives distorted figures. The limited effects of the modern impact on these countries are to be seen in the fact that, on the average, they have only one radio for every 750 people and one doctor for every 42,000 people. The process of urbanization has hardly begun; only about 5 per cent of the population lives in cities of over 100,000 people. The rate at which people are being trained in new skills is extremely low: only about 15 per cent of the primary school age students are attending school, and only a handful of men have received a university education.

In most neo-traditional countries the first prerequisite of political development must be the establishment of modern structures of administration and government. Those neo-traditional countries that were once under colonial control generally experienced indirect rule and are now without even the typical colonial administrative heritage. The basic framework of modern governmental agencies is missing, and the concept of public administration through a professional civil service is generally unknown.

The neo-traditional oligarchies still reflect the ancient practices of confusing and combining administration and politics. Government and politics in such countries are little more than the social and personal relationships among the elite class. Family ties are generally still the basic bond in political relationships. The royal family is the central political unit in Cambodia, Laos, and Nepal, in Saudi Arabia and Jordan, and only slightly less so in Ethiopia and Yemen. It is often from within these very families that the strongest pressures for modernizing arise. Out of their associations with foreigners and their exposure to modern education and modern urban life, many of the younger members of such families become intrigued with the possibilities of improving their societies.

Historically there have been examples of members of a traditional elite serving as the prime agents of modernization. The need they have felt to preserve the integrity of the state against foreign pressures has sometimes been the opening wedge for policies of radical change. Beginning with the need for armies and military technicians, it has soon become apparent that these shields of the country must be supported by other modernizing agents. Taxes must be collected to support the emerging state apparatus, and this calls for a more modernized civil service.

The process of political development in neo-traditional oligarchies quite clearly revolves around the replacing of traditional bonds of social organization and allegiance with new bonds which are more functionally distinct and which can better represent the interests common to a developing country. In some countries, such as Yemen and Jordan, this means that the patterns of loyalty among tribal chieftains must be replaced by loyalties to a state and the impersonal instruments of control. In other examples, such as Laos and Cambodia, the suzerainty type of relationship between those who dominate the capital city and those who hold power in the provincial centers must be replaced by more explicit, more durable ties which will be administratively more efficient and politically more sensitive. In other countries, such as Iran, the crucial question is how the bonds of monarchy can cope with, or even survive, the tension between the old and established rural landed interests and the emerging urban constellation of interests. If the landed interests resist change, dissatisfactions in the rural areas are likely to erupt in the form of restless immigration into cities which cannot absorb such increases in the supply of labor. On the other hand, a premature breaking-up of the landed gentry's power base before an alternative power structure has become effective can easily lead to mob rule, a situation which nondemocratic elements are certain to exploit.

Regardless of these variations, the basic problems of the neo-traditional societies are remarkably similar. In all these countries the question is whether the traditional bonds of social and political organization can, and will, be effectively utilized to usher in the essential preparation for modernization. If such preparation is not made, the pressures for modernization will operate on the society in such a way as to produce social disintegration, which in societies that have never developed complex and powerful organizations can be of such an order that only the most extreme measures of reorganization are of any consequence. The fact that historically traditional forms in many different societies have been able to control and channel the introduction of new techniques and technologies suggests that the extreme pattern of social disorganization is not an inevitable one for the neo-traditional oligarchies. Indeed, the recognition of the need for modern administrative methods and modern political forms by the current leaders of these countries may be the best, and even the only, way they can hope to preserve the unique sentiments of their traditions.

Transitional Oligarchies

In this second group we would include most of the former colonial countries and a large number of the remaining transitional societies. For the most part these countries have formally adopted Westernized institutions of government. At the one extreme are countries like many in Africa which have only a thin layer of modernized leadership and extremely fragile Western structures of government. At the other extreme are countries like Pakistan, Burma, Thailand, or Vietnam in which the dominant elite element is in full command of national power but faces tremendous problems in changing the rest of the society. Thus this group includes both newly emergent countries with disturbingly few trained leaders and countries in which there has been an overproduction of Westernized intellectuals.

These countries share a common goal—in a sense, a common mood. The leadership in each of them seeks to develop a strong, prosperous state along modern lines and at the same time to preserve the unique qualities of the traditional society. Thus the basic issue is the adaptation of institutions of Western origin to local conditions. Moreover, they present a common picture of social tension. They have made an early commitment to representative institutions of government, but despite apparent widespread support of nationalistic symbols, they have not yet created a genuinely national political process. Beneath the Westernized leadership, parochial and sectional loyalties remain extremely strong. As a result, they tend to be inherently unstable societies in which the uneven process of change and disruption is dominant and where peoples' ambitions for a new life run far ahead of their abilities to perform effectively in a modern world.

Politically, these are countries in which there is no stable and accepted system for changing leadership. Party development has not reached the point at which the people as a whole feel that they have an effective means for participating in making national decisions. In most cases, political life is dominated by a strong leader, ruling through the force of his personality.

When we try to visualize the pattern of their future political development, we should be aware of two related conditions that have dominated the pattern of change in nearly all the transitional oligarchies during the last decade. First, the demand for the fruits of modern life, whether expressed by a few leaders or by growing numbers of the people, has persistently remained far ahead of the supply. Second, there has been a steady but accelerating drift toward authoritarian practices, partly because of general dissatisfaction with the slow rate of change and partly because of the absence or weakness of institutions, interest groups, and political parties capable of resisting the organized power of the army and the state.

In various combinations, these two conditions have caused political life in most of these countries to become increasingly characterized by frustration, disillusionment, impatience, fear of failure, and uncertainty. With only a few notable exceptions, the first ten years of independence among the Asian countries have seen a decline in bold planning and in belief in heroic deeds. A rising sense of realism has brought an increasing awareness of self-limitations. In Africa the newest countries are not moving to independence with the self-confidence that was characteristic a decade ago, and among the South and Southeast Asian countries there has been an articulation of expected failure that was previously unknown.

The critical fact that emerges, then, is that in these societies there are potentially dangerous trends toward disintegration. If they are to be halted, and gradual progress begun toward stabilization and the establishment of effective democratic procedures, certain crucial problems will have to be tackled with skill and energy.

In what follows we shall discuss a few of these central tasks which apply in some degree to all the transitional oligarchies.

One of the most essential requirements is to raise drastically the number and quality of people capable of administering the society's business. It is obvious that, no matter how much outside aid is secured, programs of economic development can hardly be carried through effectively without a sufficient number of skilled administrators. Moreover, the weakness of the civil bureaucracies may cause leaders to rely more and more on oratory to maintain their grip and less and less on performance. Or, despairing of their ability to introduce reforms under the existing system, they may come to hope that authoritarian methods will be more effective. Here too they are likely to be frustrated: without the machinery to implement their constructive policies, they will be able to do little more than repress the forces working for change.

A second major need is to expand greatly popular participation in political life and so narrow the inordinately wide political gap between the highly Westernized urban leaders and the rural-based and tradition-oriented masses of the people. People out of touch with their leaders may feel compelled to look for new channels through which to express their political needs, and, in their frustration, may become susceptible to the appeals of extremist groups, including in particular the Communists. Programs for improving health and education, programs to promote land reform and raise agricultural productivity—fostered and planned in the city but carried out in the countryside—can help bring the urban elite and rural masses into a meaningful political relationship.

A third and closely related need is to create a political process that provides the means for the peaceful transfer of power. The unity inspired by a single dominant leader whose personality has been a powerful unifying force for the entire nation, or by a single party that has dominated the scene for many years, important as it is, does not constitute the whole foundation for stable political life. When the leader dies or the ruling oligarchy is split, anarchy and civil war may result unless alternative interest groups have coalesced and discovered means of expressing themselves on the political scene. Besides unity, the other prime ingredient in a stable and effective political system is its very opposite—diversity. The test of political maturity in these countries will be their capacity to accept the emergence of genuine democratic opposition that expresses the interests of different groups in the society, not merely the urge for power by different factions of the elite.

Lastly, the rationale and purpose of local welfare and improvement programs should not only be to bring the urban elite and rural masses into a meaningful political relationship but also to give citizens some sense of the role of their own initiative and individual participation in promoting the development of the nation as a whole. Where there is ignorance of the limits of government in affecting social and economic conditions, people tend to see those with political power as omnipotent and therefore wholly responsible for progress. The population may not even see itself as the necessary partner in developing the society, and hence the very spirit of public life may be one of rejecting the need for sacrifice and sustained effort in creating the nation. In such circumstances the combination of unrealistic expectations and sense of frustration may undermine the initial commitment to democratic institutions.

The tasks facing the modernizing oligarchies are thus formidable and complex. But the problems they imply are not insoluble. Nor are they necessarily beyond the capabilities of the existing and potential leaders if encouragement and the necessary resources, both tangible and intangible, are made available.

The Actively Modernizing Oligarchies

These are the most advanced of the underdeveloped societies, where there may still be considerable numbers of traditionally oriented people but where the main focus is on maintaining and operating modern institutions. In these countries there is a broad enough leadership to provide some sense of stability and continuity, and in some of them elections have brought a transfer of power without undue violence.

Such countries as Turkey, Brazil, and Mexico seem to be well on their way to becoming modern societies. Others, such as Malaya, India, the Philippines, and Colombia, are, so to speak, poised on the brink of sustained commitment to modern practices.

The central task in these countries is to maintain and accelerate the pace of economic and social development, to encourage the existing favorable trends and insure that physical limitations and resource shortages do not so impede development as to drastically disrupt the progress already under way toward modernization.

Although many of these societies present considerable ground for hope, it should be recognized that the present pattern of their social and political development by no means guarantees an inevitable march toward the acceptance of democratic institutions. History demonstrates that there is no neat correlation between the degree of democracy in a country and the degree of economic and social modernization. Severe strains at various points could lead to the reversal of present trends in a democratic direction and even to the acceptance of openly authoritarian systems. Recent events in Turkey provide some clues as to the factors that might operate to push these societies at least temporarily in authoritarian directions. The alternative between communism and democracy may be even more sharply posed in these societies than in societies with a more traditional political setting. Since traditional values and institutions have already been deeply eroded, success in the modern sector is all the more crucial to stability.

What is required if these societies are to move toward the achievement of a viable national system of democratic political procedure?

One underlying requirement is that they generate a high degree of consensus not only that modernization should occur but also as to the appropriate ends and legitimate means of political activity as a whole. With such a consensus, although controversies over the relative roles of public and private enterprise, for example, may well persist, they will arise within an accepted framework of political practice. With such a consensus, the issues of modernization tend to become basically questions of degree. By what specific methods should modernization be pursued? At what pace? How should its costs and its gains be distributed?

The key to understanding the political process at this stage lies in the relationship between economic progress and political change. Modernization of the economy is likely to have significant political consequences. Economic progress increases the pace of urbanization, introducing a larger proportion of the population to the essentially modern set of relationships that characterize city life. Urbanization of course brings with it many problems for those forsaking the more secure and still traditional structure of village life; but over a period of time the new urban dwellers tend to accept their new functional role in the society, enter groupings that diminish the loneliness of urban life, and begin to organize and to seek to influence the political process.

Economic modernization also tends to strengthen certain elements in the political elite. It increases the number and enhances the confidence and influence of men from commerce and industry, of civil servants, and of technical and professional groups engaged in modern activities. These groups acquire a vested interest in the enlargement of the modern sectors of the society and in forms of political organization which are stable and which give them an increased voice in the society's political process.

As modernization progresses, the various elements of the political elite begin to develop relations of sufficient mutual confidence among themselves to permit the balance of political power to shift without the defeated groups regarding the defeat as a surrender of their place in the society. Viable democratic institutions begin to emerge. Various private interests within the society organize themselves and compete through the intermediary of political parties seeking power according to the principle of every man's right to vote. Participation in the political process becomes increasingly widespread throughout

the society, and men's loyalties go not merely to the particular
party faction to which they belong but to the political system
as a whole. Such a pattern of evolution presupposes the emergence and acceptance of rules of law that are able to transcend
shifts in the balance of power.

These are some of the developments that may occur in the
political sphere as economic modernization takes hold, and that
must occur, in one form or another, if democratic political
practices are to take firm root in these rapidly changing societies.
But, as we shall find frequent occasion to stress, it is in no sense
foreordained that the modernization process will yield a full-
fledged democratic system even after a society has achieved
sustained economic growth. Germany between 1871 and 1914,
for example, developed virtually all the prerequisites of a
democracy; but the power of the autocratic monarchy remained.
Russia before 1914 went some way toward creating the prerequisites for a modern democracy and was subjected to increasingly heavy pressures to alter the Tsarist political structure in
democratic directions. But power was seized in November 1917
by a self-perpetuating dictatorship, and although the modernization of Russian society under communism has evidently developed many further prerequisites for political democracy, Russia remains governed by an autocratic one-party system. On the
other hand, in societies where the modernizing oligarchy was
less firmly rooted in power (for example, Argentina) or where
it actually included among its objectives the gradual democra-
tization of the political process (for example, Mexico and Turkey), we are able to see how modernization of the society can go
hand in hand with the emergence of increasingly democratic
political practices by a process not unlike that sketched above.

The Goal of Political Competitiveness

Our discussion of political development has been strongly
informed by our understanding of democracy, and it may be
well at this stage to make explicit the relationship we see
between political development and democracy. To begin with,

we wish to avoid appearing to suggest that the transitional societies should or necessarily will develop into countries having essentially the same political institutions as the Western democracies. We are, however, keenly aware of the strong desires of most of the leaders of transitional societies to achieve democratic ideals of government. We are equally sensitive to their desires to maintain the unique identities that their traditional cultures have given them.

Clearly the problem of political development is not to realize replicas of Western institutions in all the transitional societies. It is rather to realize the functional equivalents of the essence of democratic government and politics. Specifically this seems to mean the development of more open societies which can satisfy the contending interests of their people while preserving their community identities. We are using the term "political competitiveness" to suggest the functional equivalents of democracy, that is, to denote a situation in which different interests can legally contend for a fair share of influence and control over the important decisions of the society.

In terms of the political process, then, one central test of development toward democracy is the degree of competitiveness permitted to all who would be legitimate participants in the defining and executing of the society's business. We have noted how in traditional societies all power was monopolized by a closed elite. We have also noted the typical absence of groups with specific, limited, and negotiable interests. It seems likely that as the processes of social, economic, and psychological change continue to operate on transitional societies they will produce ever widening ranges of political interests and increasing numbers of would-be political participants. These processes of change can and sometimes do lead to a host of pathological, social, and political reactions. On the other hand, they can also provide the basis for a genuinely pluralistic society in which the individual may make honest choices as to what he would be and what he would have his country be. Politically this means an ever expanding degree of competitiveness so that the stability of the society will no longer have to depend upon the will of an authoritarian government, but may instead arise out of the firmer web of the overlapping interests of free groups composed of free men.

The degree of competitiveness thus becomes a question of, first, the extent to which interests are fully articulated and political parties are independently organized; and, second, the extent to which the stability of the society stems from the vigor and integrity of the struggles for office and for public policy alternatives.

There are two main types of semi-competitive political systems. First, there are those with many of the forms but without the substance of an open political system; they may have political parties, but the opposition parties are constantly harassed and suppressed. Second, there are semi-competitive systems in which the forms of an open system are missing but the group in power is visibly seeking to introduce the basic conditions of a democratic society. This type includes countries under the domination of a single nationalist party which is performing a tutelage role and also the terminal colonial countries which are being prepared for independence.

There is no deterministic pattern guaranteeing that countries will move from traditional authoritarian systems to semicompetitive ones and then eventually become fully competitive. The crucial point is that the social, economic, and psychological forces of modernization can prepare the ground for such a pattern of development. These are the forces that can make possible the development of an open and pluralistic society of free men. However, these forces, in isolating people from the security of their old associations and in creating a more impersonal social environment, can also prepare the ground for people to find a new sense of security in the massive, diffuse, and uncompromising character of totalitarian movements. The process of modernization thus sets the stage for a struggle between the alternatives of freedom and totalitarianism; hence, our concern that political development be coupled with increasing degrees of competitiveness.

Implications for Policy

PART II

Implications for Policy

Chapter Seven

THE THIRD CHOICE

WE HAVE EMPHASIZED the great complexity of the process of social, political, and economic change through which all the societies we refer to as underdeveloped are passing. The complexity results partly from the fact that modernization involves interaction among psychological, political, social, economic, and cultural factors and partly from the fact that the histories, traditions, resources, and values of the various countries of the underdeveloped world are very different. The process of continuous interaction among so many variables in so many different circumstances would be impossible to trace and to describe with precision even if all the variables could be described in mathematical terms and each assigned a firm statistical weight. Obviously, in dealing with men and societies, neither the qualitative relations nor the quantities can be firmly and unambiguously established.

Nonetheless, sufficient common elements can be discerned to allow some generalizations about the American and free-world interest in the forms taken by the transition process in the modernizing nations and to permit the identification of some broad guidelines for policy toward those nations. As with any simplification of highly complex phenomena, such generalizations will do violence to some of the characteristics of each case. However, although in designing specific policies it is essential that the unique features of each country be taken fully into account, there is need as well for an overview to guide the philosophy and general direction of policy. To provide such a perspective is the purpose of this chapter.

Perhaps the most pervasive element in the modernization process is the profound and progressive widening of men's perceptions of the realistic alternatives open to them, sometimes referred to as the revolution of rising expectations. Too frequently the term has been used as if it referred exclusively to expectations in the economic sense, to newly perceived possibilities of consumption and standards of living which in traditional societies men would have regarded as wholly unattainable. Such new perceptions do indeed exist, but there are also more profound and far-reaching changes in men's views of the world and of the individual's place in it. Men begin seriously to contemplate new values, new forms of political organization, new kinds of careers, new access to knowledge, new relations with those who have traditionally been their superiors, their inferiors, and their peers. They perceive new patterns of social organization, new possibilities of movement, new kinds of leisure.

The pace varies, but this widening of perceived alternatives is universal and inevitable. Three forces tend to start it and keep it moving: widened contact and communication with more modern societies, the rise of trade and of cities, and the emergence of new generations born into a world where modern activity is increasingly a fact of life rather than a perceived break with the past. The widening of perceptions occurs first among a limited element of the elite of the society, especially those exposed through education, government, or commerce to life outside the traditional society. It gradually spreads to wider segments of the population until it becomes a popular rather than an elite phenomenon; and today there is almost no backward segment of the most traditional society which has not been to some degree touched by this process, though its more massive consequences still lie ahead.

The movement toward modernization sets up many opposing political, economic, and social currents within traditional societies. Previous chapters have analyzed some of these in detail; our present purpose is to suggest in necessarily simplified fashion the consequences for policy of the conflict between traditionalists and modernizers that underlies the process of change in all these societies.

On the one hand, the process of modernization is profoundly disturbing to all those deeply committed to the traditional society. They may fear that it will deprive them of the power, respect, affection, income, or security afforded them by the traditional way of life. Moreover, the traditional leadership may see the new aspirations as imposing on them responsibility for new kinds of activity which they have neither the resources nor the skills to carry out successfully. They are likely to pay lip service to modernization in recognition of its attractions to others, but, especially if they feel that they cannot effectively promote it without danger to their own position and interests, they are likely to attempt to divert attention from it by stirring up other issues and to repress its advocates.

On the other hand, those growing groups to whom modernization is attractive will be seeking with mounting insistence for ways to promote it. The forms their pressure for modernization takes will depend on how rapidly and how effectively the sectors of society with which they are most intimately concerned appear to be moving in the right directions. If existing institutions appear to be pliable enough, if change is being fostered with some competence, and especially if those with new aspirations are themselves being given opportunities to participate actively in the modernization process, they may accept gradual evolution as a tolerable path toward their new goals. But if their aspirations are being frustrated, if the leadership is rigidly traditional, or incompetent, or opposed to change, and if the new aspirants are being given no role to play in building a new society, they may well conclude that their aims can be advanced only by violent overthrow of the whole existing structure. In such circumstances extremist philosophies like communism, arguing that violent revolution followed by authoritarian control is the only route to modernization, will have great appeal.

That such a sequence of events is a real possibility is suggested in varying degrees by the recent histories of Cuba, Egypt, and Iraq. Each country was ruled for a substantial period by a repressive government whose power was based on landowners and other conservative elements linked to the traditional society. The regimes of Batista in Cuba, Farouk in Egypt, and Nuri Said in Iraq thus generated in time revolutionary reactions directed simultaneously against the powerful classes in the society and against the agricultural and commercial interests which, in association with foreign influence, dominated the domestic scene. But these and other revolutionary movements have themselves often been transformed into regimes as authoritarian as those they have struggled to displace. Why should this so often have been the case?

Much of the answer lies in the fact that the old regimes had harshly suppressed moderate reform movements, killing their leaders or driving them into hiding, exile, or passivity. Such repression gradually convinces the mass of the people that they can place no hope in moderate movements for reform. Increasingly they may tend to find emotional satisfaction in nothing less than extreme and violent opposition to their rulers, in following fanatically a leader who promises to deliver them from oppression. A revolutionary movement, moreover, tends to develop an authoritarian dynamic of its own. If it is to succeed in such conspiratorial circumstances, it must often develop a highly disciplined and hierarchical style of organization which may influence the structure of its rule over the country once the revolution has taken place. In addition, a repressive framework of political activity tends to draw into underground revolutionary activity individuals who themselves are characterized by one type of authoritarian personality. One common trait of this type of personality appears to be a tendency to see a mortal threat in any rival power and to feel safe only when possessing undisputed supreme power, or when following a leader with such power. Such personality types seek to make their way to positions in which there is no competing authority, and the governments they set up in the name of liberty tend, in a familiar historical pattern, to be authoritarian ones.

But this is only one of many possible patterns. The essential point is that the course which each underdeveloped society takes will depend heavily on the realistic choices which various influential members of the society see as open to them.

One possibility is likely to be seen as the preservation of many features of traditional society, the maintenance of the existing hierarchy by repression if necessary, the destruction of forces promoting change, and perhaps the diversion of dissatisfaction through external adventure. Another will certainly be perceived by some as the radical destruction by extremist measures, probably involving violence, of the whole political, social, and economic fabric of the traditional society and its replacement by something entirely different.

If both traditionalists and modernizers view these two choices as the only ones open to them, tension and conflict are almost inevitable, and the prospect for modernization under democratic forms of consent is remote. Those in power, having everything to lose by revolution, become increasingly obsessed with devices to retain and solidify their power in the face of the mounting pressures for change. Because the sheer maintenance of authority absorbs their energies, they are unable to devote consistent attention to modernization even when they accept its desirability. In the long run they are doomed because time steadily swells the ranks of the opposition. Those who are discontented, with a decreasing stake in the existing order and nothing to lose from its overthrow, focus increasingly on the revolutionary discipline necessary for an attempt to seize power and decreasingly on how to use it constructively once they have it. If they do acquire power, they take over a society which is demanding modernization but which has few of the required institutions, skills, or resources. In these circumstances the dispersion of decision-making and initiative so essential to democratic modernization is too dangerous to the new leadership, and they either retain power by the same techniques by which they acquired it or are forced to yield to yet another revolutionary group.

But these two choices, fortunately, are not the only ones men perceive. There are almost always some traditionalists and some modernizers who, with varying degrees of clarity and hope, perceive a third choice—the gradual modification of the institutions, practices, and structure of the traditional society in the direction of modernization while retaining some of its traditional cohesive features.

The third choice is also a conditional one. If progress is too slow, if opportunities to participate in promoting it are too limited, if existing institutions cannot adapt in time, there will be widespread frustration and disenchantment with this alternative. On the other hand, if the forms of modernization are adopted more rapidly than they can be made to function effectively, then traditional values, institutions, and gratifications will be destroyed before modern substitutes have been developed, and again the third choice will be unacceptable. The extent to which this evolutionary choice continues to be regarded as attractive and realistic by major segments of the society depends upon the rate at which effective modernization occurs in each segment as compared to the rate at which aspirations there are changing.

*   *   *   *

This summary review of the major alternatives perceived by men in transitional societies can be related to the interests of the United States and the rest of the free world in the evolution of the underdeveloped nations. From this perspective, our over-all objective can be described as an effort to maximize the attractiveness and feasibility of the third choice: to help make the evolution to modernization successful enough that major groups will not struggle either to repress change entirely or to promote it by ruthless and extremist measures.

These general objectives can be viewed from the perspective of each of the interacting psychological, political, economic, and social forces of modernization.

In a psychological context the fundamental interest is that the peoples of the underdeveloped countries perceive constructive alternatives both to regressive clinging to old values and to radical overthrow of those values and an ill-considered and desperate rush to totally new ones. The danger is that the old gratifications will lose their stabilizing appeal before new ones have been developed to take their place. As the old ties weaken, men must be offered opportunities to shape a new identity and a new image of a meaningful life in the performance of new and constructive functions. Throughout the society opportunities must be created for individuals to find political, economic, and social roles in aspects of modernization which give them a psychological stake in its continued success.

Politically the guiding interest is that chaos, tensions, and failure do not lead people to accept a repressive concentration of power in the hands either of a traditional elite or of a revolutionary dictatorship. This means that as increasing numbers of people become politically conscious they must see opportunities to exert some influence on the political process and on the decisions that affect their lives. This condition cannot be assured merely by the imposition of democratic forms. Indeed, in societies with little experience of decentralized authority and little consensus on national goals, too rapid a delegation of power is a sure route back to repressive authoritarianism. Where traditionally the individual has had little opportunity to shape his own destiny, the third choice requires the development of a wide range of activities that bring home to each group a sense of its responsibility for building its own future in the context of a wider loyalty to the society as a whole. For constructive political evolution to occur, these new activities must touch all aspects of life, not only politics. Public and private institutions of all sorts must be established to provide a framework within which these activities can take place.

Our objective can also be considered from the standpoint of social structure. In the early stages of modernization the perception of both the possibilities and the dangers of modernization are likely to be found mainly in small elite groups—the traditional feudal or tribal leaders, the military, the initially small but growing urban commercial and business class, the landowners, and the intelligentsia. As the process takes on momentum and the perception of new alternatives spreads through the society, new groups become important—the peasantry, urban labor, the new student class. If evolution is to proceed in an orderly fashion, each of these groups must come to perceive the practicality and attractiveness of the third choice.

Finally, there is the economic dimension. If the economy does not move forward, the prospects for progress in other areas will not appear bright. Economic progress must be regarded both as a result of a movement toward modernization on other fronts and as a force making for further change. Economic progress needs, for example, a minimum group of modern men in the society before it can begin; and the expansion of modern economic activities itself trains more such essential men. Similarly, a certain degree of effective central direction is required before economic progress can get well under way; and a central government gains in efficiency, authority, and stability by the very act of taking effective leadership in economic development. Economic progress requires a dispersion of initiative and decision-making to a growing number of groups throughout the society; and economic progress itself creates new kinds of professionals, new urban technicians, new initiatives among the peasantry, new attitudes toward saving, and a new mobilization of capital resources for productive purposes. Economic progress itself also generates both the new attitudes and the new resources which permit such progress to continue. Finally, the phase of take-off, if successful, not only consolidates the capacity of the society to grow regularly but also tends to consolidate the political, social, and psychological benefits of modernization.

Thus the problem of making the evolutionary third-choice alternative seem both real and attractive is one with many facets. It is useful to look at it from the varied perspectives of the psychologist, the political scientist, the sociologist, and the economist; but it is one problem, not four. If action from the outside is to influence the choice, those wielding the various instruments of international policy must see the problem in these terms and see it whole, since each instrument affects the whole course of a society's evolution.

* * * *

By way of summary, we may refer to the four objectives suggested in the Preface as representing the basic American interests in the transitional process.

First, the emerging nations must be able to maintain their independence, especially of powers hostile or potentially hostile to the United States. We have noted that if the third choice appears unlikely to effect progress toward meeting the goals of important groups, conflict is almost certain to result between regressive forces of tradition and groups that see their only hope in the violent overthrow of these forces. The former may triumph for a time, but cannot do so indefinitely. The latter will not hesitate to seek support where they can find it, notably from powerful countries which themselves have an interest in instability and in the overthrow of "bourgeois" regimes. In this period of history the Communist powers are more than eager to assist revolutionary movements, at the price of subservience to their own broader international goals.

The second interest is in the emergence of states that do not resort to violence in their external relations. Traditionalist leaders, unwilling or unable to contain disaffection by promoting internal change, have historically tended to engage in external adventure as a distraction. New revolutionary dictatorships likewise, unable to cope effectively with the popular demands they have helped to stimulate, have a similar motive for aggression. Although modernization does not by any means eliminate the possibility of an aggressive external policy, it does lower the probability of erratic and irresponsible adventurism in foreign affairs.

Third, it is in the American interest to see the emerging states maintain effective and orderly governments without resort to totalitarian controls. Regimes, whether traditional or revolutionary, which cannot at least partially satisfy the rising demands for modernization on the part of all important groups can maintain order only by increasingly repressive measures. It is a necessary condition for attaining the other objectives, therefore, that the developing societies be capable of progressively meeting the aspirations of their people.

Fourth is the interest in seeing states emerge which accept the principles of an open society and which are willing to cooperate in international economic, political, and social control measures. Neither of these conditions is likely to be met by a dictatorship, regressive or revolutionary, which has confidence neither in the loyalty of its own people nor in its own capacity to deal with either external or internal forces. Evolutionary and balanced progress toward modernization will not assure behavior in the American interest, but it is a necessary condition for such behavior.

It should be noted that we have not explicitly listed the defeat of communism as a fundamental objective of American policy in the underdeveloped countries. That objective is clearly implied in the positive, constructive, and more fundamental interests we have defined. Communism is only one of the alternatives to the third choice, and there are other dangers we should not overlook. Nonetheless, at the present moment in history it is an alternative so important that it deserves a special word.

It is now widely understood that the essential appeal of communism is not, as Marx believed, to advanced, modernized societies. As economic growth has become a permanent condition in capitalist, democratic societies, it has proved possible to distribute the fruits of modernization so as to avoid the bloody class conflicts on which Marx counted and to avert the progressively more acute crises of unemployment which he believed would inevitably lead advanced societies into communism.

Both historically and at present the appeal of communism has been strongest in societies caught up in the cross currents of the transition from traditional to modern status. What communism has to offer such societies is a political and social method which promises these things: first, a tight, unified organization of some of the elements of the elite who wish to modernize the society; second, a domestic base of power capable of defeating those elements from the traditional society who would maintain regional authority or otherwise oppose the modernization process; third, a technique for mobilizing the human and physical resources required to produce rapid industrial growth; fourth, a psychological setting which gives a framework of security, discipline, and order to men cut adrift from the moorings of the traditional society.

In short, communism develops one kind of urban-based, modernizing elite which can lay claim to the task of carrying modernization through its decisive phase. It appears as one form of political organization capable of launching and sustaining the growth process in societies where there has not developed an adequate political consensus among the leaders of the society or an effective program of modernization. It is not strange, then, that communism as a technique for organizing men and resources should appear attractive in the face of the confusions and distractions of the transitional stage.

It must not be overlooked, however, that the image of communism also has strongly negative aspects which have caused men to resist its adoption in the underdeveloped countries. First, communism has been unable to free itself from its direct connection to Moscow and, more recently, Peking; it therefore encounters resistance from the spirit of nationalism and nationhood. Second, Communist parties are built on a relatively narrow segment of the modernizing elite and are therefore forced not only to struggle against elements from the traditional society but also to compete against those who would press toward modernization by other methods and under other banners. Third, there are deeper resistances than some Western observers are aware to the definitive violation of democratic hopes and commitments which the acceptance of communism involves. Put another way, the democratic vision is often more influential in transitional societies than a casual view of the low estate of democratic practice would suggest.

Nevertheless, two things remain true in contemporary underdeveloped areas. First, communism is an active competing alternative to other methods of organizing the society for modernization—an alternative not only alive as a political party but also alive in the minds of non-Communists as they weigh the possibilities for progress against their frustrations. Second, a portion of the modernizing elite in most underdeveloped areas is committed to the Communist course and must be counted on to frustrate and complicate the efforts of others to move toward modernization by methods that hold open the possibility of a democratic evolution for their society.

Chapter Eight

INFORMATION AND
MILITARY ASSISTANCE POLICY

WE TURN in this and the following chapter to three principal instruments of foreign policy, the increasing importance of which is a comparatively recent development imposed by relations with the new and underdeveloped countries. These are information and cultural exchange, military aid, and economic and technical assistance.

Information Policy

We have noted that the spread of knowledge about modern ways and a desire for their benefits can be anticipated universally and with certainty, that the revolution in ideas and information is one of the dynamic forces in the transition process. It follows that the instrumentalities of information and communication may play a vital role in the execution of our foreign policy in transitional societies. The major objective of our information effort in underdeveloped areas should be the spread of useful information about modernization. The adoption of such an objective would be a major departure from present

105

policy, which seeks primarily to create a favorable image of the United States.

An information agency has no one exclusive purpose. It is an organization characterized rather by a distinctive expertise in mass media techniques. Its staff are competent on such matters as radio and motion picture production, the local practices of press coverage and news-story filing, the details of voluntary associations and influence networks. This expertise is there to be put at the service of foreign policies whatever they may be. Thus the goals of a nation's informational effort are those of foreign policy as a whole. The creation of a favorable image of the United States is certainly among the legitimate purposes of our information efforts abroad, but not the first objective. Moreover, it is a purpose which can seldom be effectively served directly. If people in underdeveloped countries find that American visitors, American books, magazines, and reference materials, American libraries, and officials are interested in the things which seem important to them, and that these American activities work effectively in helping them reach their own goals, a favorable attitude will result. The dissemination of laudatory statements about the United States and the American way of life seldom has the desired effect.

It is hardly necessary to stress the extent to which American and other Western missionary and civil educators have contributed to the development of the new elites in what were once colonial and semi-colonial countries. They left a profound impact on the attitudes, manners, and values of men who now occupy the most responsible positions in their societies. The anti-Western nationalism of many of these educated elites should not lead us to underestimate their deep attachment to many aspects of modern life. Rather, nationalistic and hostile reaction to the experience of Western education and to Western ideas should impress on us the fact that programs of information and education do not cause people to abandon their natural loyalties or to develop an unmixed affection for their teachers. Ambivalence and sensitivity characterize the attitudes of transitional elites. They want contact with the modern world, but they also want respect for their own values and cultures. Western education, Western books, and many other things which we take for granted are craved, but not if the price is a sense of inferiority. We shall compound the difficulties of relations with the newly emergent countries if we fail to take full account of their sensitivities toward the symbols of their subordinate past or toward their new aspirations.

The legitimate purpose of our information policy in underdeveloped countries is to help produce in their people a better understanding of the modernizing process in which they are participating. Information programs should help provide the kinds of knowledge which may help to ease the inevitable private anxieties and public crises associated with modernization and thus improve the chances of a stable and democratic evolution. As a result of such efforts, respect may indeed be won for Americans and for American institutions which are seen to contribute to the underdeveloped country's own efforts; but this can be only a by-product. By contrast, efforts to awaken admiration for the United States which do not simultaneously contribute to the needs of the countries themselves tend only to increase the jealousy and resentment that so often result from the gulf between the modern and the less developed world. Too often, for example, we have displayed the American standard of living and American consumer goods where they have no relation to the feasible objectives of those to whom they are shown. Of infinitely greater value are young people's exchange programs and other endeavors in which Americans work side by side with the people of underdeveloped countries in trying to meet development goals. Such programs have the value of bringing people together not in a relationship of hierarchy where one advises and the other obeys, but in a relationship of common effort. There are many problems about any exchange program— such as getting sufficiently able and mature people, finding suitable tasks for them, overcoming language deficiencies. We shall not discuss those here. Suffice it to say that on balance the net effects of our exchange programs with developing countries, both programs bringing visitors to the United States and those taking Americans abroad, have been decidedly favorable. Most particularly, the results have been favorable when the nature of the programs has been that of common effort to reach goals meaningful to those with whom we were working.

What, then, can an American information effort do in developing countries? We note four important functions it can serve. It can present non-Communist alternatives for development, provide a medium for technical assistance information, help develop the mass media and cultural activities, and act as the eyes of the world upon the country's development.

Communism offers itself to the modernizing literate urban strata in underdeveloped countries as a way of life which will make things better. We need to publicize ideological alternatives. Unlike the Communists, we do not have a fixed doctrine which we aim to sell, but we can in each country seek out those local values and aspirations which are consonant with our own democratic orientation. Among these shared values are respect for religion, science, and economic progress. It is just as fitting for our information effort to offer facilities to a Buddhist international congress as to a lecturer from the United States; to offer facilities for a local science fair as to arrange a visiting exhibit of American science; to show in Africa a movie on the successes of Indian development plans as to show one on the American economy.

It follows that the American information program should be among other things an information service for technical assistance. The highly successful information services of the Marshall Plan provide a model. Their activities in support of productivity teams and of anti-Communist labor leadership were among the great successes of America's postwar information effort. Our current programs in developing countries can learn from that experience. United States Information Service libraries and film libraries can become resources of great importance to countries without adequate reference institutions of their own. Technical information centers could be established in major African and Asian cities. U.S.I.S. staffs in underdeveloped countries should therefore include a substantial proportion of persons who are competent in technical matters.

The information services have a special competence in one area of development where they can do more than be a reference service. In the development of mass communication systems they can perform functions which would otherwise be assigned to other development agencies. For example, our information specialists overseas might run training institutes for movie or radio technicians, or courses in press operations. They might help writers and artists form agency organizations to get their material to publications in the United States and abroad. They might help organize village radio systems or help in the establishment of libraries.

Such activities are more than marginal frills in a development effort. The mass media bring new aspirations and wider perspectives to developing countries. They provide the psychic spark to modernization. They help weld the diverse elements of a traditional society into a nation, for they substitute for the oral channels within familial or tribal groups, new uniform channels reaching the whole nation. They provide the means whereby development planners can mobilize the whole populace for purposes of agricultural improvement, public health, or education. Thus mass media are an important part of the social overhead capital of a developing country.

A major breakthrough for development would be the creation and production by the millions of a cheap long-lived battery radio or television set designed to bring mass communication into villages, bypassing the prerequisites of literacy and electricity. That is feasible, and American efforts can help. Also helpful would be measures to raise the professional status of mass media personnel. One cannot expect the cast-offs of better paid professions, frequently unemployed intellectuals, men without security, to provide a constructive responsible national voice. The values, aspirations, and quality of media personnel will be translated into the character of a nation's development process. American information specialists abroad can seek to give to their media colleagues in the countries in which they operate opportunities for respect and accomplishment via fellowships, organizational cooperation, seminars, education, publication, recognition, and so on.

Lastly, the information program can promote stable and progressive evolution in a developing country by informing its people about the attention and respect the world is giving its progress. This is not a trivial matter. People all over the world are eager for news about how others regard them. The American press in its foreign reporting pays great attention to attitudes of foreigners toward the United States. The Berlin press during the blockade satisfied the avid desire of the Berliners to be assured that the rest of the world knew about and appreciated their effort. So too in underdeveloped countries there is great sensitivity to what others think about them. An election in an underdeveloped country is much more likely to be conducted in a fair and democratic manner and to come to be regarded as really valuable if it is felt that the West is watching with interest and approval. A hundred correspondents from the Western press arriving to report the election would have a profound effect. Respectful articles printed in the West should be disseminated back to the country concerned. Such feedback can be a powerful weapon against corruption, factionalism, or dictatorship.

In summary, the development of the communication industries and of communication and educational facilities should be top-priority national programs, and American informational and investment efforts should contribute to them. Student and other exchanges should be increased, especially in ways that result in joint effort toward achieving the goals of modernization. Above all, we must judge the results of our efforts not primarily by the development of attitudes favorable to us but by the development of attitudes which contribute toward a stable democratic development of the modernizing societies.

Military Assistance Policy

This study does not concern itself extensively with military matters. We are assuming that the United States will maintain both an invulnerable strategic air capability and a conventional force capability sufficient to convince the Communist powers that we have the means and the will to respond to limited aggression by limited means. We shall here deal with American military policy only to the extent of suggesting some of the ways in which military measures may contribute significantly to furthering the constructive process of modernization which it is in the United States interest to promote.

The primary task of American military assistance is to help protect societies from invasion or from internal subversion by an armed minority supported by an outside power. Particularly in the early stages of the transition process, when leadership groups contend among themselves for power and central governments are likely to be weak, societies are acutely vulnerable to invasion or civil war. The postwar history of Asia has shown clearly how realistic is the threat of Communist military action against weak or divided states. But postwar experience in the Philippines, Burma, South Vietnam, and Malaya has also demonstrated that if such societies can be effectively protected from a Communist conquest during their most vulnerable stage, they may well find their feet, consolidate their nationhood, and begin to move forward toward modernization. Although each of these countries has a long way to go, its present status would have been predicted only by extreme optimists at the peak of its crisis period.

While American military aid can thus contribute materially to the preservation of independence and the encouragement of political stability, the United States should not give military assistance to a repressive regime. Such a government may for obvious reasons be particularly eager to form an alliance with the United States and receive military aid. The short-term gains which the United States might derive from such an association should not be allowed to obscure its consequences in the long run. Ultimately such a repressive regime will be overthrown, and, if the United States has been too closely involved in its support, the ensuing government and the people as a whole may well be hostile to the United States, rejecting our help in the development of their country and forming alliances which threaten our interests.

What we would particularly emphasize is that in addition to assisting in the relatively conventional military task of defense, American military assistance properly administered can have a strong constructive influence on the evolution of the transitional

societies. The potential positive contributions of military aid
have been too little noted or applied, partly because of the
inadequate coordination of American programs. We have looked
at military assistance too much from the point of view of its
military effectiveness alone; its relationship to social, economic,
and political change, and to the over-all policy objectives of
the United States in the transitional societies has been given
too little consideration.

There are two broad areas in which local military forces can
make valuable contributions to the course of modernization.
First, they can contribute directly to major tasks of economic
development, particularly the building of certain sorts of social
overhead capital. Second, they can assist in training large numbers of people in the skills and attitudes demanded by a society
undergoing social and economic transformations in the direction
of increased urban living and industrialization.

The army in an underdeveloped society often contains a high
proportion of the men trained in orderly administration and
in the handling of modern technology. The army also generally
controls substantial amounts of transportation, communication,
and earth-moving equipment. Without sacrificing military effectiveness, army units can be used on major development tasks
such as road or dam construction, building of communication
systems, irrigation and land reclamation, and surveying. American military missions should not only encourage local military
forces to assume responsibility for such projects but should also
help provide the equipment which they require. There is every
reason to assist the military to play the kind of constructive role
in their society that the Army Corps of Engineers played in the
modernization of the United States, particularly in the first half
of the nineteenth century.*

---

* For further reference see the study prepared for the President's Committee to Study the United States Military Assistance Program. Entitled
"Contributions of Military Resources to Economic and Social Progress,"
this study explores in some detail the ways in which the United States can
raise the economic and social potential of foreign military forces and lists
some of the nonmilitary activities in which foreign military groups are currently involved. *Annexes*, Volume II of the Composite Report of The
President's Committee to Study the United States Military Assistance Program, Annex D, p. 121.

The second area in which the military can make a major contribution is training and education. The period of military training affords the opportunity to make the soldier literate, to teach him basic technical skills, and to inculcate in him such basic attitudes as the respect for authority and organization which are essential to modern life. The army can be a highly significant training ground for large numbers of men, preparing them for new roles in society. The United States should stand ready to help design and to provide generous financial and technical assistance to programs likely to have an important long-run impact on the level of skills and attitudes in the army and in the society as a whole.

Officer training is another important task in which the United States could play a more useful role than it has in the past. Opportunities should be expanded for foreign officers, especially at the middle and junior levels, to travel and study in the United States. Moreover, the programs we set up for officers when they are in this country should not be exclusively devoted to technical military matters; we should encourage them to think and talk about such broad problems as civil-military relations, the potential uses of the army in economic and social development, the economic and political evolution of their country as a whole.

The tradition of military life in the transitional countries, especially among the older generation, is to remain aloof from nonmilitary activities; but circumstances in the past few years have tended to break down this tradition, and the officer corps in many countries has become steadily more involved in economic and political life. In a number of countries it has assumed at least temporary control of the government. Inevitably, therefore, the officers have become much more acutely aware of the problems attending modernization, and they are likely to respond positively to vigorous and sustained American efforts to raise their own capacity and that of the military as a whole to deal with these problems.

Deeper military involvement in economic and social activities may well have the further consequence of bringing the army into closer union with the entire society. Traditionally, the military tend to be regarded by the people as a distant elite force which absorbs their taxes and recruits their sons. The sense of nationhood and of common national purpose would be vastly strengthened if the military joined in the constructive tasks of modernization. Such closer linking of the soldiers and the people can also have a military significance. In many areas the most likely form of war is internal insurrection aided from abroad and conducted along guerrilla lines. The outcome of guerrilla operations often hinges on the sympathy and support of the peasantry, who have it in their power to deny information and supplies to either side. The use of the military establishment in constructive enterprises at the village level can create close working links between the soldiers and the peasants.

Chapter Nine

ECONOMIC POLICY

THE FUNDAMENTAL ROLE of American and free-world economic policy in the modernization of the underdeveloped countries is implicit in the nature of the transition process. The degree and kind of economic assistance these countries receive will inevitably influence the design of development efforts and their effect on evolution in the political and social as well as the economic sphere.

Here we shall consider four aspects of economic policy: technical assistance, allocation of capital, assistance to land reform, and the international organization of aid.

Technical Assistance

Although technical assistance programs do not require as large budget allocations as capital expenditure and loan programs, their potential influence in shaping the evolution of developing societies, especially those in the early stages of transition, may well be decisive. Moreover, their management requires a level of administrative attention and competence quite out of proportion to their dollar cost.

The immediate function of technical assistance programs is to

115

bring the knowledge and skills available in the developed countries to bear on the problems of modernization. Techniques and methods which will enormously increase productivity can be transferred in agriculture, education, health, administration, small-scale enterprise, construction, transport, and communication. Great care must be taken, however, to assure that the techniques to be applied are appropriate to the physical conditions, resource endowments, social environment, economic organization, and cultural pattern of the recipient country. Technical knowledge can rarely be transferred unadapted from a developed to an underdeveloped country. Although this fact has been increasingly recognized in research on development problems and in the many new training programs for technical assistance personnel sponsored in recent years, the scope of American research and training efforts is still far too limited and the tours of duty of technical assistance experts frequently too short.

The second major objective of technical assistance programs must be to develop to the fullest the human resources of the recipient country. This goal can be achieved partly by assisting formal educational programs, but it should animate all technical assistance activities, even those having no explicit training component. Through their behavior in the foreign society technical assistance experts may not only transmit technical skills and expertise to those with whom they are working but also in subtle ways influence motivations, attitudes toward change and innovation, perceptions of alternatives, and the like.

Human resource development may often require more than advice and training from abroad. Foreigners of all ages and skills may be needed to fill certain operational roles in the society—as teachers, administrators, extension workers, engineers, economists, public health workers—until such time as the supply of qualified indigenous personnel can meet the minimum demand. Investment in people is a type of capital formation with unusually long gestation periods, and if development is not to be slowed down by a shortage of skilled and experienced men and women, the gap must be filled by human imports.

To give this dimension of technical assistance its full effect, we should know a great deal more than we presently do about what kinds of investment in human resources are most needed in each underdeveloped country. Much more extensive and detailed studies are required of the prospective supply of and demand for men with a variety of different skills. The dangers of training men inappropriately are as great as the dangers of not training them at all. If educational goals, curricula, and procedures based on the practices of developed societies are applied hastily to underdeveloped areas, the result is likely to be a class of educated unemployables who may be the most disruptive element in a transitional society. To be effective in developing the kinds of human capital most needed, technical assistance experts in all fields must have a deep understanding not only of the economic but also of the social and cultural needs of the people in the countries to which they are assigned.

A third goal of technical assistance programs should be to help close the gap between the small urban elites who have taken the first steps toward modernization and the large groups in the population, especially in the countryside, whose expectations are rapidly changing. One criterion for the selection of technical assistance activities should be the degree to which they offer opportunities for as many groups in the society as possible to participate in the modernization process. Agricultural extension programs, local public works, assistance to small-scale enterprise, and other such activities provide rich opportunities for the urban leadership to become involved in the daily problems of all segments of the population. The need to stimulate this kind of interaction and communication among the different parts of a transitional society should be borne in mind in designing technical assistance programs.

A further major objective of technical assistance should be to help build permanent institutions which can eventually assume full responsibility for the functions for which outside help was initially asked. The most effective way to help build such institutions is not to provide special experts in public administration or business management, though they may have a role to play, but rather to imbue the technical expert in each professional field with a realization that institution building is at least as important a part of his mission as the transfer of special knowledge. Each specialist should regard it as one of his primary objectives to develop an institutional situation in which the need for further technical assistance will be minimized and in which the indigenous experts trained will have the greatest chance of making their activities operationally effective. A related goal should be to build greater confidence among the emerging professional groups of the underdeveloped society so that they can deal with their own problems without leaning heavily either on the overtaxed central political leadership or on continued help from abroad. These objectives require much more subtle and extensive training than most technical assistants assigned to field missions now receive.

Finally, it is important that technical assistance should be handled from the start in such a way as to convey an image of American purposes, intentions, and modes of operation which will lay an effective basis for future cooperation as assistance programs expand. This image will be conveyed most powerfully not by high-level speeches about American foreign policy but by the day-to-day behavior of the many kinds of technicians we dispatch for assistance activities. To accomplish this objective, like the others, technical assistance personnel must acquire a subtle and sophisticated understanding of the problems and sensitivities of the people with whom they are dealing.

Allocation of Capital

The broad purpose of capital assistance is to encourage the recipient countries to maximize their own efforts toward development. Its effectiveness depends not only on the amount and kind of assistance made available but also—and importantly—on the terms and conditions under which foreign capital is offered.

For capital assistance to have the maximum leverage in persuading the underdeveloped countries to follow a course consistent with American and free-world interests, that assistance must have certain characteristics:

1. The economic criteria on which development capital is made available must be clear and unambiguous, and we must be firmer than we have frequently been in the past in the application of those criteria.

2. The offer of capital on terms requiring the recipient to meet conditions for its productive use must be held out consistently over long enough periods of time to permit the incentive effects to work. Such a result cannot be expected from programs with no more than one or two years' assured life.

3. The amounts offered must be large enough and the terms flexible enough to persuade the recipient that the game is worth the effort. This means that we must invest substantially larger resources in our economic development programs than we have done in the past.

4. The kinds of capital we offer and the purposes for which we encourage it to be used must be sufficiently varied so that the growth of no important sector of the economy dependent on foreign exchange will be inhibited by its lack. For example, if the use of foreign assistance is limited to social overhead or big industrial projects, bottlenecks may well develop in other sectors which will lead first to economic stagnation and then to political and psychological frustration.

5. For political as well as economic reasons the leadership in underdeveloped countries should be encouraged to formulate their development goals in national terms. At an appropriate stage in the transition they should be urged to work out and discuss widely in their countries coordinated programs or plans which will underline the relationship of individual and local effort in particular sectors to national purposes and objectives.

6. In order that recipients of aid may move as rapidly as possible toward freeing themselves from dependence on extraordinary intergovernmental assistance, they should be encouraged to relate their own economic development as fully as possible to the growth of the international economy.

These requirements are discussed more fully below.

The economic criteria for economic assistance must be unambiguous and firmly applied. We have been much too slow in shifting the criteria of American aid away from the ambiguous standards of emergency or defense support to the more rigorous standards of development lending. If, as this study contends, our most important objective in the underdeveloped countries is to promote their modernization through evolutionary processes, clearly the resources we make available should constitute an economic contribution to that end.

When governments know they are likely to receive foreign exchange assistance on noneconomic grounds, the incentive for them to face up to the development of their own economy and to increase its capacity to absorb capital is reduced. Thereby the whole modernization process is slowed down. Governments tend to accommodate themselves to situations of slow change or even stagnation, relying on American aid based on noneconomic criteria to bail them out periodically. Nothing is more corrosive of the central purpose of our assistance programs than the knowledge on the part of recipients that, if they can only generate a sufficient sense of political or military crisis, they can blackmail us into supplying financial resources without their having to take the difficult, often painful, steps required for the economically effective use of those resources. Emergency aid and temporary financial support of foreign regimes for political reasons are certainly often necessary elements of U.S. foreign policy. But the use of these types of aid should be severely limited in time and place, in contrast to development aid which should have a long horizon and be consistently available to those who meet the criteria for it.

Whether or not economic criteria are firmly applied does not depend mainly on how clearly the purposes and conditions of our assistance programs are enunciated in legislation or in high-level pronouncements, though this is important. The determining factor is the way in which those programs are administered in detail, partly in Washington but mainly in the field. Those responsible for development aid allocations must base their decisions on economic criteria rather than on considerations of short-run political advantage. In the long run our programs will be more likely to have the political consequences we seek if they are based on reasonably strict economic criteria.

Capital must be made available over sufficiently long periods of time. We can hardly encourage the recipients of assistance to take a long-run view of its purposes unless we demonstrate that we ourselves take such a view. If we want them to devote their efforts wholeheartedly for five or ten years to building the resources and institutions which will make it possible for them to utilize capital, we must persuade them that such extended efforts will yield larger resources. Past budgetary procedures have frequently had the reverse effect, stimulating recipient nations to seek grants and loans before the appropriation expires even though they were not yet ready to use them. Our development lending agencies must have substantial resources covering the potential needs of the underdeveloped countries over a long time period if the incentive effects of their lending criteria are to be fully realized.

The amounts of capital assistance must be adequate and the terms on which it is offered must be flexible. If the resources available to an underdeveloped country from outside appear to cover only a minor fraction of what is required to make a reasonably soundly based attempt at take-off, the leverage which the United States can exert with its resources will be small and its objectives will not be achieved.

The Center for International Studies in 1957 made a rough estimate of the additional foreign capital which would be needed annually to raise the rate of growth of income of all the underdeveloped countries to a level in the neighborhood of 2 per cent per year per capita. We estimated that to achieve this end the underdeveloped countries required $3.5 to $4.0 billion more per year than they were then getting from all sources. As we then indicated, however, a good many of the underdeveloped countries will not for some time create the preconditions which would permit them to absorb this amount. The actual disbursement of capital aid would, therefore, be very much lower (say two-thirds) than the appropriation needed to provide development incentives. The present limitation of absorptive capacity, which we have recently recalculated for each of the underdeveloped countries, would make it impossible for many of them to realize at once an annual rate of growth of 2 per cent per capita. We estimate the total capital inflow which these countries can absorb during the next five years at about $5.7 billion per year, of which perhaps $1.4 billion might take the form of private investment, leaving $4.3 billion to be met by governmental aid. "Aid" consists of grants and long-term loans, including two-thirds of P.L. 480 surplus products* but excluding short- and medium-term loans. Of the total aid of $4.3 billion, the International Bank and the International Development Association are likely to provide $500 million net per annum. Aid to be provided by governments should, therefore, amount to around $3.8 billion. If the United States were to bear a 65 per cent share of the burden, its aid appropriation would amount to about $2.5 billion. If we add to aid thus defined funds for technical assistance and for the emergency fund, the total United States share would amount to just under $3 billion. (See Appendix, Table V. This figure excludes both so-called "special assistance," most of which is for other than developmental purposes, and funds for social development objectives like education and health whose contribution to gross product is intangible. It also excludes defense support, although some of the aid in this category contributes to development goals as well as to the maintenance of military establishments.) The present United States economic aid comparably defined amounts to about $2 billion. It consists of:

$0.7 billion		Loans by the Development Loan Fund
0.3	"	Loans of the Export-Import Bank
0.6	"	Two-thirds of sales of surplus products under P.L. 480
0.2	"	Technical assistance
0.2	"	Emergency fund

The United States would, therefore, have to increase the amounts classified as economic development aid by around $1 billion annually over the next five years, that is, by slightly less than 50 per cent. Economic aid would then amount to about 0.6 per cent of U.S. gross national product. The contributions would

---

* It is assumed that two-thirds of surplus products offered to underdeveloped countries raise their investment while only one-third results in increased consumption.

fall slightly during the subsequent five-year period and very considerably during the next five-year period as domestic capital formation rose in the recipient countries.

If the leaders of those countries which are now able to make effective use of a substantial volume of outside resources do not see a high prospect that something like this volume of capital inflow will be available to them over a period of years, they are likely to be discouraged from taking the painful domestic measures required to develop a vigorous and successful program of modernization. As this study has emphasized throughout, the difficulties of modernization are legion, and the pressures are powerful to turn in directions contrary to American interests. Politicians will be far more inclined to pin their political futures to a program of rapid economic development without recourse to repressive measures if they can see reasonable prospects that at least one major bottleneck, the shortage of capital resources, can be broken by assistance from the United States and other countries.

Almost as important as the total amount of capital assistance are the terms on which it is made available. The period during which a net inflow of extraordinary capital will be required is long enough so that short- or intermediate-term loans impose risks of unacceptable foreign exchange burdens. A fraction of the capital requirements can safely be met by long-term, relatively low-interest loans requiring specific repayment in hard currencies. In even the most favorable cases, however, the prospects for entering the stage of self-sustaining growth will be somewhat uncertain, and underdeveloped countries will be understandably hesitant to assume firm obligations which, if their luck is bad, they may not be able to meet. It is reasonable that they should expect the developed countries to take an equity rather than a creditor's position in their future economic growth. A substantial portion of the necessary capital should therefore be made available in such a way that required repayment in the currency of the lender is to some degree conditional on the degree and pace of the growth process achieved by the borrower.

Capital must be made available for all important sectors of the economy. There is some danger that the project orientation which has characterized a good deal of development lending up to the present will fail to meet urgent requirements for foreign exchange in certain sectors of the transitional economy which may be vitally important both economically and politically. Project lending is well adapted to financing investment in social overhead capital such as transport, communications, power, and large irrigation works. It is now reasonably well recognized that the appropriate criterion for estimating the productivity of investments of this kind is not their self-liquidating character but is rather the increases in gross product of the recipient country which they may make possible. Project lending is also appropriate to supply the capital for larger scale industrial enterprises, some of which will be included in the program of most countries at the take-off stage.

Project lending cannot, however, supply all the kinds of capital required. One important form of capital which we now supply but the rationale for which is not always clearly understood is surplus American agricultural production. This is especially important in permitting an overpopulated country like India to utilize fully its own manpower resources, since, in the absence of food and fiber imports, wage payments to the unemployed for work on projects of capital formation would tend to cause local demands for food and clothing which would be inflationary. We should work out careful schemes for offering inflation insurance to underdeveloped countries as an incentive for them to utilize their own manpower and other resources more fully. In some circumstances capital assistance in the form of agricultural surpluses can sensibly represent a substantial fraction of our total assistance. It should be used more explicitly than in the past as a specific incentive to increase employment in the recipient country.

Another important requirement which will not in general be met by project financing is the provision of sufficient foreign exchange to permit the expansion of investment in the small-scale private sector of trade and business. This sector tends to be slow in emerging in the early stages of the transition, primarily because appropriate motivations and skills are lacking.

The Indian experience has shown, however, that a country approaching take-off may well exhibit quite an extraordinary flowering of initiative in the development of large numbers of small enterprises. The importance of this phenomenon is far greater than would be suggested either by the total amounts of capital involved or by the total contribution to output of these enterprises. Substantial employment opportunities are likely to be created, especially among those groups in the population most in need of constructive outlets for newly aroused aspirations. Moreover, a large middle class of small-scale entrepreneurs engaged in commercial and industrial activities which they find rewarding and satisfying can do a great deal both to promote modernization and to inhibit the growth of extremist movements.

Care must be taken to see that enough foreign exchange is available to meet the needs of this group. These needs seldom if ever take the form of substantial projects which can appropriately be submitted to foreign or international agencies. They usually consist of large numbers of very small requirements for an individual machine, a critical part, a minor imported raw material, or a small amount of foreign technical help. Such requirements can sometimes be met by supplying foreign exchange to development banks or other financial institutions in the recipient country which can then make it available to qualified entrepreneurs locally.

Finally, foreign exchange must be available to meet the working capital requirements of development, which are often underestimated by planners. As industrialization proceeds, raw materials and semi-manufactured components are required in growing volume to fill the swelling pipelines of new production. Inventories must be built up at all stages of manufacture and commerce from raw materials to retail stocks. This expansion of goods in process, which is as essential a part of capital as rolling mills and electric generators, cannot normally be financed with project loans and must be supplied in other ways.

From the discussion in Chapter Five of the relations between the public and private sectors it should be apparent that we advocate great flexibility in the supply of foreign governmental capital to both sectors. Whether particular kinds of activity should be carried on by public or private enterprises in the underdeveloped country is a question which should be determined pragmatically, rather than ideologically, by the country concerned. Our own capital assistance should be available to both.

Lastly, there may be special capital assistance requirements associated with programs of land reform; these are discussed at a later point.

National development programming should be encouraged. Development programming need have little relation to the degree of direct governmental ownership and operation in the society. In Chapter Five we made clear our reasons for believing that national coordination of the economy is necessary. Earlier chapters emphasized that one of the great problems of the newer states is to establish among the various groups of their peoples effective loyalty to the nation focused on constructive goals. These nations must develop an appropriate balance between the necessary decentralization of decision-making, power, and initiative which modernization requires and the sense of common commitment to national goals which will prevent sectional or parochial interests from destroying orderly procedures of government. National programming can be an exceedingly valuable political device for bringing home to each segment of the population the relation between its own special goals and achievements and those of the larger community to which it belongs. For these political and sociological as well as economic reasons the United States should encourage the preparation of multi-year development programs as a basis for capital assistance applications.

Development efforts should be related to the international economy. It is becoming increasingly true that the long-term viability of the economies of the newer nations depends on their finding ways of fitting their own productive resources and potential into the international economy. Although their main focus of attention, especially in the earlier stages, must be on the development of domestic institutions and market structure, they must eventually meet their growing import requirements less and less through continuing governmental capital assistance and more and more through their own export potential and their ability to attract capital inflow through normal channels.

There are four ways in which we can use our influence to these ends. The first is to demonstrate convincingly our own willingness to expose ourselves to the risks and opportunities of relatively free international trade. When the United States ties its development loans to purchases in the United States, the example it sets does serious damage. Second, we must renew our efforts to palliate some of the more serious consequences of wide fluctuations in the prices of international raw materials on which many of the underdeveloped countries are dependent for their export earnings. Third, we should encourage increased consultation and cooperation among the countries of each region in their investment programs. Particularly among groups of smaller countries great economies can be secured through the explicit tailoring of development programs to complement one another. Fourth, we can provide more effective technical assist-ance in helping underdeveloped countries appraise the potential of the key sectors of their economies.

Assistance to Land Reform

The critical role which changes in the organization of agri-culture are likely to play in the modernization of the politics, psychology, sociology, and economics of the transitional societies has implications for American economic assistance policy.

The path to modernization of agriculture through land reform is often blocked by the reluctance of large landowners to see steps taken which might alter their privileged status. At the same time, the peasants often exert strong pressure to acquire ownership of the land. The resulting conflicts are complicated by the fact that land reform schemes taken by themselves are unlikely to increase agricultural productivity. They may even result for a time in a decline in productivity as the number of small and relatively inefficient holdings increases, and in a decline in food deliveries to urban areas as the new landowning peasantry raises its food consumption.

It is evident that the American influence on the outcome of these deep-seated problems can be only marginal. Nevertheless, several specific prescriptions are possible. First, where a government is prepared to take the leadership in land reform, American policy should strongly back that effort not merely with normal diplomatic support but also by helping to mount programs of technical and capital assistance to the peasants which will link land reform to substantial increases in agricultural productivity. Second, American food surpluses should be used to cushion any temporary decline in food deliveries to the cities which might result from land reform. Third, the United States should use whatever influence it has with the large landowning groups to interest them in the modernization process. Historically, the social conflicts inherent in modernization have been reduced when the large landowners have begun to raise the productivity of their own land or when they have shifted their interests to commerce and industry. Fourth, if governments wish to buy out the large landowning interests as part of a land reform scheme, the United States should seriously consider the possibility of providing financial assistance for the purpose.

The International Organization of Aid

It is often noted that the increasing number of aid instrumentalities in an increasing number of donor countries is posing serious problems of coordination. Each borrowing country must deal with a bewildering complex of national and international agencies offering different kinds of assistance under different terms. To coordinate the efforts of all these potential sources of assistance so that they can fit in most constructively with the development plans of each nation is a difficult but nevertheless urgent task.

In approaching the issue of coordination, discussions of international economic and technical assistance frequently focus around the possibility of channeling aid through a single international organization. It is our view that to lump the existing agencies together, creating a single international pool of capital, would be neither a feasible nor a desirable solution.

In the first place, it is doubtful that the United States Congress and the parliamentary bodies of the other lending countries would grant sufficient resources to such a pool to make a serious dent on the development problem. It is true that legislative bodies might be encouraged to increase their contributions for international economic assistance when they observed other nations making substantial contributions. Such a possible benefit could also result from looser forms of international coordination where each nation pledged a certain amount but retained control over the allocation of its own resources. The essential drawback is that legislative bodies are likely to resist voting large amounts of tax money to an international aid organization over which they can subsequently exercise little influence. They are likely to insist upon retaining sufficient control to be satisfied that the money is being efficiently administered and that reasonable criteria for its use are being maintained.

Second, it cannot be assumed that each donor country has identical objectives in supplying economic aid or that its contributions are qualitatively identical to those of other countries. Each country may have a variety of special interests which it hopes to further, depending on its geographical or strategic position, its historical ties with one or another of the newly independent countries, and its assessment of the relative potential for development of different countries. Different resource endowments or trade patterns may also make donor countries able to contribute most effectively to the development of certain countries. The aid allocations of Japan will be different from those of Canada, those of France from those of Great Britain. A delicate adjustment must be reached between the interests and potentialities of each supplier and those of each recipient.

A third consideration is the persistent tendency to create new international institutions without abolishing the old national ones. Since it is doubtful that countries will be willing to put their development activities entirely into the hands of an international agency, existing national institutions will not readily be abandoned; the creation of a single international aid agency might result in further confusion rather than simplification of aid channels.

The task of simplification is two-sided. The lending countries must be able to get a more accurate picture of the over-all needs of the underdeveloped countries if they are to arrive at some reasonable allocation of the burden among them. The borrowing countries must in turn have a more efficient means of discovering the nature and amount of the resources available to them from various sources. We would hold that what is lacking is not a single unified organization to administer all economic assistance but appropriate machinery for coordinating the various national and international agencies now operating. There are several distinct aspects of the problem which we shall briefly consider.

Most important is coordination within each national unit. Economic development is basically a job each nation must do for itself. No amount of international machinery can substitute for well-developed programs at the national level and for the weaving into these programs of all the various types of external assistance available. In the end, whatever the superstructure for international institutions, these require the method of the consortium, in which the men responsible locally sit down with responsible men from other countries and work out a program for action. The task of the consortium is to bring to bear on a national development program all the instruments available to each donor nation: food and fiber surpluses, hard loans, soft loans, technical assistance, and private capital.

The second level of coordination is regional. The possibilities for this kind of cooperation vary radically with each area. In the Middle East, for example, a number of possible joint investment projects can be conceived, perhaps utilizing oil revenues contributed on a regional basis. In Latin America possibilities exist for trade and currency agreements and for cooperative arrangements between public and private capital. In the Colombo Plan, investment-trade arrangements like the Indian-Japanese pig iron deal can be made. In Africa many possibilities exist for cooperation between newly independent states and their former European metropoles. The important thing is that if regional arrangements are to be strengthened they must be strengthened by developing a lively sense of the limited concrete issues which can sensibly be discussed in regional terms. Regional institutions have a role to play, but they are a substitute neither for national nor for international agencies.

The third kind of coordination required is among those furnishing capital and technical assistance. The new Organization for Economic Cooperation and Development holds high promise of serving this purpose, since it offers the opportunity for a new European relationship with underdeveloped areas on a basis other than colonialism and of avoiding an excessive concentration of European capital in residual colonial areas. When such a free-world organization of suppliers demonstrates its effectiveness, a standing invitation to participate should be issued to each of the Communist bloc countries.

Whatever the locus and membership of the lenders' group, its agenda should include: the examination of fair shares in international lending; appropriate criteria for lending; the apportionment of technical assistance in ways to maximize the special advantages of each potential donor; the interweaving of public and private capital; the long-term funding of short-term debts; the coordinate use of food and fiber surpluses; and preliminary arrangements for *ad hoc* consortia.

Fourth, there is a need to provide a forum in which donors and borrowers can get together periodically, exchange complaints, survey results, and make commitments to be worked out in detail at another time. The lenders' group might take the initiative for such gatherings.

Thus American policy should be prepared to move in four directions toward coordinating loans and technical assistance: toward strengthening the new O.E.C.D. as a special forum for lenders; toward the creation of an over-all forum for lenders and borrowers; toward expansion of regional programs based on concrete possibilities for regional cooperation; toward enlarged use of the consortium technique as a method for bringing to bear on the development of each country all that the international community can effectively provide.

Chapter Ten

SOME GENERAL IMPLICATIONS
FOR POLICY

IN CONCLUSION, we turn to consider a few important general policy implications of the changes involved in the modernization of traditional societies.

In view of the historical limits of foreign policy, perhaps the most fundamental implication to be brought out is that the United States and other developed nations must accept and openly declare their interest in the internal stability and development of other nations. They must declare their hope of influencing the course of evolution of other nations with the consent and active participation of those nations themselves.

The traditional premises of international relations were a product of the European nation-state system within which differences in culture and technology were not great. The concept of a community of nations implied the tacit acceptance of a set of standards and principles of action, such as nonintervention in the domestic affairs of other societies in the community, conduct of diplomacy according to certain formal rules, and use of alliances against common dangers. The concept of national sovereignty presumed that governments were able without qualification to commit their people to whatever international obligations they saw fit to make.

The entrance of the new and underdeveloped countries as actors upon the international scene has brought many of these principles into question. Can relations among societies continue to be limited primarily to the formal relations among governments? Should the new governments be expected to meet the type of commitment traditionally accepted by national governments? Can the presumption of unconcern about internal developments in other nations be maintained when a primary international activity must be the transferring of talents and skills, including those of administration and policy-making? And when there is a gross difference in levels of technology, can the obligations of alliances be shared equally?

Such questions make clear the need to create a new system of international affairs which can provide an acceptable basis for relationships among societies at radically different stages of development. International policy must be shaped to meet that need. These relationships must be grounded in a shared interest in furthering a process of modernization which will enable the transitional societies to develop their own versions of responsible government and to play a cooperative role in a new world order. To the extent that such an overlap of interest and vision can be established between the modern societies and those now in the process of transition, it must be translated into joint programs for action. In short, both parties must acknowledge that the relationship transcends that of conventional international behavior and may involve activities within other societies which formerly would have been precluded.

The Scope and Focus of Policy

From this enlargement of the basic concepts of international relations there follows the implication of a corresponding enlargement of the foreign policy function. That enlargement in turn suggests new apparatus and personnel and an unprecedented and skillfully coordinated use of the instruments of economic, military, and informational policy.

This study has reiterated that modernization is a dynamic process occurring through the interaction of the economic, political, social, and psychological forces in a society. Clearly, policy designed to have the maximum constructive influence on the course of modernization should coordinate every instrument of international policy. It should employ them in a way for which traditional practices offer no precedent. As far as possible, military, economic, and informational programs should be fused into a coherent design for each country. Persistent efforts should be made to explore the ways in which the separate arms of policy might contribute to achieving our over-all objectives in the transitional societies.

It is not our purpose here to offer specific prescriptions for policy toward the many countries with which we are concerned. Nevertheless it has seemed useful to attempt a few generalizations about priorities which should be kept in mind in designing programs for countries at various stages of evolution from the traditional state. In so doing, we have arbitrarily divided the field into three categories of societies, roughly equivalent to the neo-traditional, transitional, and actively modernizing groupings employed in Chapter Six. Any such classification does not of course alter the fact that the detailed operational plans which implement policy must take into account the particular needs of each society.

Neo-Traditional Societies

In societies still close to the traditional stage, where the impetus to change has begun to gather strength but only very limited numbers of the elite have been exposed to the modern world, the highest priority need is to build up human resources— both by educating and training individuals and by creating modern economic and political institutions. This applies to most of Africa south of the Sahara, to the more backward portions of the Middle East, and to certain of the less advanced areas of Asia and Latin America.

In these regions primary education, teacher training, and vocational institutes thus comprise one set of urgent needs. At the same time, emphasis is required on technical and administrative training for the elite groups who must direct the modernization process, such as the nucleus of a national civil service and a core of men who can guide the transformation of agriculture. Much of the effort in these fields can be initiated and promoted, as in the past, by various American private and voluntary associations. Governmental assistance is also needed, however, in part because it can more readily encourage the emerging leaders to think in terms of the needs of their society as a whole. Efforts should be made not only to assist in the establishment and initial guidance of the required training activities but also to encourage these countries to keep educational opportunities open to individuals from as many groups in the society as possible.

The effort to create a broader and more competent elite needs to be balanced by investment in general citizenship training. There is a great danger that educational programs will leave the masses of the population untouched while producing an increasingly alienated elite class of men who cannot perform effectively in their own national environment. The elite will remain isolated and ineffectual unless the rest of the community begins to both contribute to and benefit from the process of modernization. It also frequently happens in countries at this stage that national leaders, who may themselves be some distance removed from the grass roots of their societies, may attempt to move rapidly toward modernization along conventional Western lines without fully appreciating the violence being done to the desires and traditional ways of their people. Educational programs and other means which help establish better communication between the urban elite and the rest of the people can pay large dividends.

The societies at this early stage of transition are not ready for comprehensive development programming or the application of large capital sums. They lack political cohesion and the administrative and technical skills to implement and supervise an extended program of investment in capital goods. The sense of national entity has yet to prevail. The aim of our economic aid policy should thus be to help create the minimum social overhead capital necessary for the economic and political unification of the nation. Programs relatively small in size, if skillfully and sensitively administered, may exert great influence both on the process of national unification and on the degree to which we can be helpful at later stages when there will be opportunities for more substantial assistance programs. Technical assistance programs should make particular efforts at this stage to help the local governments survey systematically their priority tasks and the resources available for performing them. This is the time to help establish a wide variety of data-collecting and statistical-reporting procedures—surveys and projections of manpower, education, health, agricultural conditions, and resource availabilities. Such surveys should place major emphasis on training people and on establishing procedures which will enable the recipient countries to perform national survey functions regularly on their own initiative. They can be designed to serve a double purpose: to provide essential information to the new governments and to put us in touch with a large number of elements of the indigenous society. They will be crucial to more ambitious development efforts later.

These societies can expect to face difficult times. As the historic processes of modernization gradually gain momentum, their cohesion will be threatened by divisive forces, the gaps between rulers and subjects, town and country, will widen; new aspirants for power will emerge whose ambitions far exceed their competence; old rulers may lose their nerve and their sense of direction. National leaders will have to display the highest skills of statesmanship to guide their people through times of uncertainty and confusion which destroy men's sense of identity. Feelings of a community of interest will have to be recreated— in some of the new nations, indeed, they must be built for the first time—on a new basis which looks toward the future and does not rely only on shared memories of the past. Nevertheless, with foresight and careful planning, some of the more disruptive and dangerous consequences of social change which have troubled other countries passing through this stage can be escaped. The United States can help by communicating a genuine concern with the problems these countries face and a readiness to provide technical and other appropriate forms of assistance where possible.

Our central goal should be to provide the greatest positive incentive for these societies to tackle boldly the tasks which they face. At the same time, we should recognize that the obstacles to change and the lack of cohesion and stability which characterize these countries may make them particularly prone to diversions and external adventures of all sorts. It may seem to some of them that success can be purchased much less dearly by fishing in the murky waters of international politics than by facing up to the intractable tasks at home. We should do what we can to discourage this conclusion, both by offering assistance for their domestic needs and by reacting firmly to irresponsible actions on the world scene. When necessary, we should make it clear that countries which choose to derive marginal advantages from the cold war or to exploit their potential for disrupting the security of the world will not only lose our sympathy but also risk their own prospects for orderly development. As a nation, we feel an obligation to assist other countries in their development; but this obligation pertains only to countries which are honestly seeking to become responsible members of a stable and forward-moving world community.

Transitional Societies

When we look at countries like Iran, Iraq, Pakistan, and Burma, where substantial progress has been made in creating a minimum supply of modern men and of social overhead capital, and where institutions of centralized government exist, we find a second category of countries with a different set of problems and hence different priorities for policy. The men in power are committed in principle to modernization, but economic and social changes are proceeding only erratically. Isolated enterprises have been launched, but they are not yet related to each other in a meaningful pattern. The society is likely to be characterized by having a fairly modernized urban sector and a relatively untouched rural sector, with very poor communications between the two. Progress is impeded by psychological inhibitions to effective action among those in power and by a failure on their part to understand how local resources, human and material, can be mobilized to achieve the national goals of modernization already symbolically accepted.

Most countries in this second category share the difficulty of having many of the structures of a modern political and social system without the modern standards of performance required to make them effective. In these rapidly changing societies there is also too little appreciation of the need for effort to achieve goals. The colonial period has generally left people believing that government can, if it wishes, provide all manner of services for them—and that with independence free men do not have to work to realize the benefits of modern life. For example, in accordance with the fashion of the times, most transitional societies have announced economic development plans of varying numbers of years; such is the mystique of planning that people expect that fulfillment of the plan will follow automatically upon its announcement. The civil services in such societies are generally inadequate to deal competently with the problems facing them; and their members often equate a government career with security and status rather than with sacrifice, self-discipline, and competence.

American policy should press constantly the view that until these governments demand efficiency and effectiveness of their bureaucracies there is not the slightest hope that they will either modernize or democratize their societies. We should spread the view that planning and national development are serious matters which call for effort as well as enthusiasm. Above all, we should seek to encourage the leaders of these societies to accept the unpleasant fact that they are responsible for their fates. Only within the framework of a mature relationship characterized by honest appraisals of performance can we provide telling assistance. With respect to those countries whose leaders prefer to live with their illusions, we can afford to wait, for in time their comparative lack of progress will become clear for all to see.

Our technical assistance to these countries should place

special emphasis on inducing the central governments to assume the role of advisor and guide which at an earlier stage foreign experts assumed in dealing with the central governments. We should encourage the governments to develop their own technical assistance to communities, state and provincial governments, rural communities, and other smaller groups, making certain that no important segment of the economy is neglected. Simultaneously we should be underlining the interrelationships of technical progress in various fields, showing how agricultural training can be introduced into education, how health affects labor productivity, how small business can benefit the rural farm community, and, above all, how progress in each field relates to national progress. Efforts such as the Community Development Program in the Philippines have demonstrated that transitional societies can work toward balanced national development. To achieve this goal of balanced development, communications between the central government and the local communities must be such that the needs and aspirations of the people themselves are effectively taken into account. If modernization programs are imposed from above, without the understanding and cooperation of the people, they will encounter grave difficulties.

Land reform is likely to be a pressing issue in many of these countries. It should be American policy not only to encourage effective land reform programs but also to underline the relation of such reforms to the economic growth and modernization of the society. As an isolated policy, land reform is likely to be politically disruptive; as part of a larger development effort, however, it may gain wide acceptance. It should also be recognized that the problem of rural tenancy cannot be solved by administrative decrees alone. Land reform programs need to be supplemented with programs for promoting rural credits and technical assistance in agriculture.

Lastly, governmental and private planners will at this stage begin to see large capital requirements looming ahead. By holding out prospects for external capital assistance, the United States can provide strong incentives to prepare for the concerted economic drive necessary to achieve self-sustaining growth.

Actively Modernizing Societies

At a third stage in the modernization process are such countries as India, Brazil, the Philippines, and Taiwan, which are ready and committed to move into the stage of self-sustaining growth. They must continue to satisfy basic capital needs; and there persists the dual problem of maintaining operational unity around a national program of modernization while simultaneously decentralizing participation in the program to wider and wider groups. But these countries have made big strides toward developing the necessary human and social overhead capital; they have established reasonably stable and effective governmental institutions at national and local levels; and they have begun to develop a capacity to deal realistically and simultaneously with all the major sectors of their economies.

On the economic front, the first priority of these countries is to mobilize a vastly increased volume of resources. Several related tasks must be carried out if self-sustaining growth is to be achieved. These countries must formulate a comprehensive, long-term program covering the objectives of both the private and the public sectors of the economy. They must in their planning be able to count on at least tentative commitments of foreign capital assistance over periods of several years. Capital imports drawn from a number of sources must be employed and combined skillfully enough to permit domestic investment programming to go forward. Capital flows must be coordinated with national needs and planning. Finally, a balance must be effected among project finance, utilization of agricultural surpluses, and general balance of payments support.

Thus, although the agenda of external assistance in the economic sphere are cumulative, and many of the policies suggested for nations in the earlier stages remain relevant, the basic purpose of American economic policy during the later stages of development should be to assure that movement into a stage of self-sustaining growth is not prevented by lack of foreign exchange.

There remain many political and administrative problems to

be solved. For one thing, although considerable numbers of men have been trained, bureaucracies are still deficient in many respects; even the famed Indian Civil Service is not fully adequate to the tremendous range of tasks it has undertaken. Technical assistance in training middle- and upper-level management personnel is still needed in many cases. There are also more basic problems. This is the stage at which democratic developments must take place if the society is to become an open community of creative people. Nevertheless, impulses still exist among the ruling elite to rationalize and thus to perpetuate the need for centralized and authoritarian practices. Another great danger is that the emerging middle class will feel itself increasingly alienated from the political leaders who still justify their dominance by reference to the struggle for independence or the early phase of nationalism. The capacity of intellectuals and members of the new professional classes to contribute creatively to national development is likely to be destroyed by a constraining sense of inferiority toward both their own political class and their colleagues and professional counterparts in the West. Particularly when based upon a single dominant party, governments may respond to such a situation by claiming a monopoly of understanding about the national interest. Convinced of the wisdom of their own actions, and reassured by the promises of their economic development programs, governments may fail to push outward to win more and more people to the national effort, becoming instead more rigid and inflexible in their policies.

American policy toward such societies should stress our sympathy for the emerging social and professional classes. It should attempt to communicate both an appreciation of professional standards and an understanding of the tremendous powers and potentialities of genuinely open and pluralistic societies. We have every obligation to take seriously their claims to being democratic and free countries; we also have, in consequence, the duty to appraise realistically and honestly their performance and to communicate our judgments to their leaders in frank but friendly ways.

The Time Factor

We have emphasized that the modernizing process in each society will take a considerable period of time. With the exception of treaty-making, foreign relations were historically concerned for the most part with conditions of short or at least measurable duration. Foreign policy now takes on a different perspective and must become skilled not merely at response but also at projection. American and free-world policies can marginally affect the pace of transition; but basically that pace depends on changes in the supply of resources and in the human attitudes, political institutions, and social structure which each society must generate. It follows that any effective policy toward the underdeveloped countries must have a realistically long working horizon. It must be marked by a patience and persistence which have not always been its trademark.

This condition affects not only the conception but also the legislative and financial support of foreign policy, especially in the context of economic aid. As the previous chapter has suggested, perhaps the most serious weakness in the American economic assistance effort has been the failure to put American aid programs on a genuine long-term basis. The conventional short-term approach deprives the donor nation of the opportunity to offer powerful incentives to recipients to put their economic affairs in better order. Indeed, it has been the American experience that the rush to commit funds by the end of a fiscal year has sometimes pushed recipients into premature commitments.

The failure to adjust our policies and procedures in this respect has affected more than our economic programs; it has colored the entire American relationship with the underdeveloped countries. The United States has been engaged in assistance programs of a variety of sorts for over a decade, and there is now a fairly firm consensus that it will be so engaged for some years to come, yet legislation authorizing these programs has continued to be enacted on a year-to-year basis. This practice not only involves considerable waste of money and human energies but also greatly lessens the effectiveness these slow-acting programs could have. The very nature of the transitional process requires that foreign policy be conceived in a new time perspective.

Prediction and Policy

There follows from all of the above the implication of heightened unpredictability of results. The vastly broadened objectives and time range of policy toward the underdeveloped countries, combined with the complexity of the process which that policy seeks to influence, inevitably imply both a degree of risk of failure and a limitation on external influence not encountered with conventional foreign policy objectives. The essence of the policy-maker's task is to weigh the effects which today's acts are likely to have on tomorrow's world; policy is, in this sense, prediction. Consciously or unconsciously, assumptions must be made not only about the shape of the world as it is today, in itself no mean task, but also about its shape in the months and years to come.

Such assumptions have been made in this book, some explicit, others not. We have posed some large questions: in what directions are the presently underdeveloped societies moving, and with what consequences for the United States and the rest of the free world? Implicit in such questions, and in the use of such words as "transitional" and "modernizing," are some basic assumptions which we have asserted rather than proved—that is, that these societies are indeed going through a process which will produce in them social and economic changes parallel to those which have occurred in modern Western states, and that this process will have profound consequences for the rest of the world. These assumptions seem to us to provide a legitimate framework for our inquiry. As generalizations they appear entirely plausible, though we by no means intend to assert that the change we foresee is bound to take place rapidly, or that these societies will evolve into carbon copies of the Western nation state, or that they will all end up very much like each other. On the contrary, we expect both great variety and novelty. We live in an age when revolutionary innovation seems certain to be the rule, not the exception.

Those who study the underdeveloped countries, and who derive from their researches the moral that the West must move vigorously to assist these countries during their revolutionary transformations, have frequently been challenged for adopting too easy and optimistic a tone about the future. They have been chided for appearing to make too casually the large assumption that a sufficient quantity of economic and technical assistance, administered in a sound fashion and with the proper encouraging attitude, would go a long way toward transforming underdeveloped countries into stable and viable modern states sympathetic to the free world. Such an assumption may indeed appear to have been uncritically accepted at times, largely perhaps because the proponents of an active foreign policy toward the transitional societies have tended to focus their analysis on the economic aspects of development alone, rather than on the process as a whole. This tendency has helped to establish what Rupert Emerson has referred to as ". . . one of the cheerful illusions of our day that economic and social development will surely redound to the benefit of the West."

It has become increasingly clear with the passage of time that such illusions must be put aside, particularly to the extent that any hint of inevitability is involved. Although it does seem certain, barring nuclear catastrophe, that economic and social change will occur, it is by no means sure that these changes will result in the emergence of political systems which behave in ways compatible with Western interests. The prospect of the future is for many more situations like those in the Congo and in Laos. Even countries which may appear stable at this moment are likely to experience increasing strains as the previous order of society dissolves more rapidly than a new one can be constructed. The process of disintegration may be faster than that of reconstruction. This is why it is important to stimulate positive developments at the earliest moment possible.

As this discussion implies, to the extent that we take the interests of the free world as our frame of reference, it is the political consequences of the transition process with which we are in the first instance concerned. Our actions as a nation must be directed principally toward encouraging other nations to act in ways which do not jeopardize our values and our national security. This should not be taken to mean, however, that the "national interest" in any narrow sense should be expected to provide the exclusive motive for our actions. We have a strong moral interest as well in seeing economic and social development proceed in ways which allow other people to realize values which we believe are common to all mankind; and this moral concern has often been a powerful motivating factor in American behavior. The fact is that these common values can be realized only in the stable and peaceful world which it is our ultimate objective to achieve and which can be achieved only through political means. In the short run as well, our essential political objectives in the underdeveloped countries do not clash with our national sense of what is right. As long as our policies are designed to help these societies develop in directions which meet the real interests of their own people, our political and our moral interests coincide.

At this point we should perhaps make explicit a further assumption critical to our train of thought, namely, that close connections exist between a nation's foreign policies and its over-all domestic situation. Thus domestic economic and social changes are by no means irrelevant either to a country's internal politics or to its foreign affairs. We have attempted throughout this volume to suggest some of the relevant interrelationships, while recognizing with some frustration that as yet rather little has been systematically discovered about them. Much further work will be required before the relationships between economic and social growth and political evolution, both domestic and foreign, can be spelled out with anything approaching precision.

Are we then whistling in the dark? Are actions designed to speed up and channel the course of economic and social development nothing more than acts of faith? The pessimists may be inclined to urge that they are precisely that—that to prod and poke these modernizing societies into a more rapid rate of development may in fact bring disaster by upsetting traditional ways before modern ones have taken sufficient hold to preserve a modicum of stability and order. Or, in another mood, they may argue that we grossly overrate our influence, that the revolutionary process of change will not be significantly affected one way or the other by anything the United States does or fails to do. The relationship of the Western states to the newly emerging nations, they may point out, is neither that of a nineteenth-century European power to its colonies nor that of a modern Communist power to its satellites; no direct control can be exerted, and influence can only be marginal and indirect. Faced with such risks and limitations, it may be better to abstain entirely, to avoid becoming involved.

Some of this may be true, but none of it is conclusive with respect to policy. The skeptics are right that external influence is limited, that considerable risk of failure is involved, that more rapid rates of modernization may in the short run raise rather than lower the level of discontent and social disorganization. Our present state of knowledge does indeed require us to go at least part way on faith when we assert that an intensive and prolonged program of assistance by the free world will materially raise the chances that the underdeveloped societies can pass through the transitional period without throwing the world ever more deeply into turmoil. But not even the skeptics find it easy to argue that because of all the uncertainties these countries should simply be left alone. To suppose that stability can be maintained on the world scene by leaving them to their own devices requires an even more transcendental act of faith and a capacity to ignore the record of the past. Furthermore, it takes a gross misreading of the contemporary world to believe that these countries can in fact be left alone. Everything we do, whether or not aimed directly toward them, is bound to have consequences for their development; modern economic and political relationships among nations make this inevitable. If we should attempt to withdraw, we should not succeed in entirely removing our influence, and other societies with a better comprehension of the world would move in to enlarge theirs.

One of the more convincing lessons of recent times is that nations which are going through the process of modernization and unification have had a profoundly disruptive effect on the world about them. One need only review the histories of Germany, Japan, and Russia to be reminded of the way in which the world order has been upset as previously backward and relatively powerless nations have made the surge forward into modernity. The effort of China today to modernize and to assume a place under the sun is proving equally fraught with danger for her immediate neighbors and for the world at large. It would be folly to ignore the possibility that the same pattern might be repeated in other countries whose power potential may be lower but whose capacity for disruption is nevertheless great. Given the global ideological struggle and the Communist technique of seeking to move in wherever violence arises, the likelihood of large-scale conflict associated with modernization may legitimately seem greater than ever before.

But there are powerful offsetting factors as well, which give reason to hope that history need not repeat itself. One essential new circumstance is that means have begun to be worked out, in the decade and a half since the end of World War II, to facilitate to an unprecedented degree cooperation among nations. The developed countries have come to realize that it is both inevitable and desirable for the rest of the world to enter the modern era as rapidly and as painlessly as possible, and that it is far better to assist than to frustrate the process. Western colonial policies were at least partially directed toward the goal of modernization, and the more successful colonial experiments helped substantially to prepare certain societies for the modern world. But these policies were ambiguous at best, for the interests of the mother country could never wholly coincide with those of the colony; furthermore, the relationship of tutelage was at too great variance with modern ideas and aspirations to survive for long no matter how beneficent the policies may have been. In sum, colonialism did not prove to be a successful method of bringing the skills and experience of men from more advanced societies to bear on the task of transforming societies radically different from their own and disadvantaged in many respects. We are now faced with very much the same task, vastly complicated by a host of new factors which combine to demand that it be done at unprecedented speed. If modernization can be carried through with the full cooperation of both sides and with the best interests of the developing societies at the forefront, then the chances of minimizing the international conflicts which have previously accompanied the modernizing process will be markedly enhanced. If nothing is done, or not enough, there seems little hope of maintaining a world environment in which free societies can prosper.

SUGGESTED LEVELS
OF INTERNATIONAL AID
FOR UNDERDEVELOPED COUNTRIES

THE FOLLOWING SUMMARY TABLES are designed to give a rough estimate of the external capital required over the next fifteen years to produce rates of growth in the underdeveloped countries which are regarded as feasible in the light of the absorptive capacity of these countries. The tables are derived from a study by Professor P. N. Rosenstein-Rodan, entitled "International Aid for Underdeveloped Countries." No attempt will be made here to justify these figures or to indicate the procedures by which they have been calculated. Those interested in the detailed country-by-country figures on which the summary tables are based and in the sources and methodology utilized should consult Professor Rodan's study, which was published in the May 1961 issue of *The Review of Economics and Statistics.* Copies are available through the Center for International Studies, M.I.T. A few explanatory comments may, however, help to clarify the tables. For the sake of simplicity, most figures presented in these summary tables have been rounded off; slight deviations from the original estimates have occurred for this reason. All dollar figures refer to U.S. dollars.

Table I

ESTIMATED WORLD GROSS NATIONAL PRODUCT AND POPULATION, 1961

| | "Money" GNP | | Population | | "Real" GNP | | GNP per Capita in Dollars | |
	Billion Dollars	Per Cent of World Total	Millions	Per Cent of World Total	Billion Dollars	Per Cent of World Total	"Money" GNP	"Real" GNP
	(1)	(2)	(3)	(4)	(5)	(6)	(7)	(8)
DEVELOPED COUNTRIES								
Western Europe	285	20.6	261	8.7	385	22.0	1,091	1,472
Oceania	18	1.3	16	0.5	24	1.4	1,105	1,513
United States	515	37.3	185	6.2	515	29.4	2,790	2,790
Canada	38	2.7	18	0.6	38	2.1	2,048	2,048
Japan	36	2.6	95	3.2	58	3.3	383	613
South Africa	6	0.5	15	0.5	9	0.5	427	598
	898	65.0	590	19.7	1,029	58.7		
COMMUNIST BLOC								
Soviet Union	176	12.7	215	7.2	212	12.1	818	986
Eastern Europe	55	4.0	100	3.3	82	4.7	550	825
China	58	4.2	694	23.2	116	6.6	83	167
North Korea	1	0.1	9	0.3	2	0.1	105	211
North Vietnam	2	0.1	17	0.6	3	0.2	105	199
	292	21.1	1,035	34.6	415	23.7		

UNDERDEVELOPED COUNTRIES

Africa	21	1.5	206	6.9	34	1.9	100	164
Asia	65	4.7	780	26.1	120	6.8	84	154
Latin America	65	4.7	210	7.0	89	5.1	311	425
Europe	21	1.5	67	2.2	34	1.9	313	501
Middle East	20	1.4	106	3.5	29	1.7	187	257
	192	13.8	1,369	45.7	306	17.5		
TOTAL	1,382	100	2,994	100	1,750	100		

Table I. The first four columns provide information on the estimated population and gross national product (GNP) of all countries of the world in 1961. The gross national product estimates in the first column have been expressed in dollars by converting the estimates in local currencies into dollars at the currently effective rates of exchange. This procedure results in a serious underestimate of the gross national product of the low-income countries, since the domestic purchasing power of their currencies is much higher than would be indicated by their conversion to dollars at foreign exchange rates, which are influenced only by internationally traded goods and services. Accordingly, the fifth column of Table I ("Real GNP") attempts a very rough estimate of what these gross national products might be if each of the products produced in these countries were valued at the price for which it can be bought in the United States. The last two columns of the table, indicating GNP per capita, are arrived at simply by dividing the "money" GNP figures and the "real" GNP figures, respectively, by the population.

Table II

ESTIMATED DISTRIBUTION OF WORLD INCOME, 1961

	"Money" GNP		"Real" GNP	
Countries with GNP per Capita	*Per Cent of World Population*	*Per Cent of GNP*	*Per Cent of World Population*	*Per Cent of GNP*
$100 or less	50.1	8.5	0.4	0.1
($150 or less)	(57.1)	(10.2)	(26.6)	(6.3)
$101 – $300	15.7	6.1	59.9	16.6
($151 – $300)	(8.7)	(4.4)	(33.7)	(10.4)
$301 – $600	10.7	10.1	8.7	6.4
$601 – $1,200	16.7	35.3	15.1	21.9
Above $1,200	6.8	40.0	15.9	55.0

Table III

ESTIMATED INVESTMENT AND SAVINGS
OF UNDERDEVELOPED COUNTRIES, 1961

(*Million Dollars*)

	Gross Investment	Net Investment	Domestic Net Savings
Africa	2,490	1,740	1,210
Latin America*	10,630	6,840	5,950
Asia	9,060	6,010	4,590
Europe	3,910	2,470	1,890
Middle East	2,890	1,810	1,550
TOTAL	28,980	18,870	15,190

*Excluding Puerto Rico and the Virgin Islands.

Table II. This table groups the world's countries by income levels, in both "money" and "real" terms. It is derived from the detailed tables underlying Table I.

Table III. This table summarizes estimates of the levels of gross and net investment and of domestic net savings of the underdeveloped regions of the world for the year 1961. For these estimates to prove valid, a certain amount of foreign capital must flow into these countries in 1961; the amount of foreign capital assumed to flow in can be derived by measuring the difference between domestic savings and net investment.

Table IV

ESTIMATED POPULATION AND GROSS NATIONAL PRODUCT OF UNDERDEVELOPED COUNTRIES, 1961-1976

A. Population (*Millions*)

	1961	1966	1971	1976
Africa	206	223	242	262
Latin America	210	238	272	311
Asia	780	861	953	1,046
Europe	67	70	74	77
Middle East	106	120	136	153
TOTAL	1,369	1,512	1,677	1,849

B. Gross National Product (*Billion Dollars*)

	1961	1966	1971	1976
Africa	21	24	28	33
Latin America	65	79	98	122
Asia	65	80	99	123
Europe	21	25	31	39
Middle East	20	24	30	38
TOTAL	192	232	286	355

Table IV. This table gives estimates for 1961, 1966, 1971, and 1976 of the population and GNP of the underdeveloped countries in each major world area. The table is based on estimates for each underdeveloped country of the rates of growth of GNP which might be realistically anticipated if foreign capital were supplied according to criteria explained in the detailed study. These criteria relate to estimates of the absorptive capacity of the recipient countries. One of the important criteria proposed for the supply of foreign capital is that the recipient country should be making the maximum effort which can reasonably be expected to mobilize its own resources for growth purposes. In general, the estimates of absorptive capacity are based, first, on the record of the country in increasing its rate of investment in the recent past; second, on its recent record in raising its rate of savings and notably in achieving a higher marginal rate of savings than the average; and third, on a judgment as to the country's capability to organize and administer its development effort. In making the estimates some improvement in each of these respects is assumed.

Table V

ESTIMATED CAPITAL INFLOW REQUIRED PER ANNUM BY UNDERDEVELOPED COUNTRIES, 1961-1976

(Million Dollars)

A. 1961-1966

Region	Total Capital Inflow	Capital Aid	Private Investment
Africa	430	275	155
Latin America*	1,550	840	710
Asia	2,695	2,395	300
(Asia)	(2,520)	(2,240)	(280)
Middle East	640	475	165
Europe	385	305	80
TOTAL I	5,700	4,290	1,410
TOTAL II (Asian alternate)	(5,525)	(4,135)	(1,390)
TOTAL III (I minus Europe)	5,315	3,985	1,330

B. 1966-1971

Africa	605	395	210
Latin America*	1,495	585	910
Asia	2,380	1,965	415
(Asia)	(2,910)	(2,430)	(480)
Middle East	750	525	225
Europe	455	305	150
TOTAL I	5,685	3,775	1,910
TOTAL II (Asian alternate)	(6,215)	(4,240)	(1,975)
TOTAL III (I minus Europe)	5,230	3,470	1,760

C. 1971-1976

Africa	740	415	325
Latin America*	1,010	180	830
Asia	1,250	910	340
(Asia)	(2,270)	(1,710)	(560)
Middle East	400	180	220
Europe	360	185	175
TOTAL I	3,760	1,870	1,890
TOTAL II (Asian alternate)	(4,780)	(2,670)	(2,110)
TOTAL III (I minus Europe)	3,400	1,685	1,715

*Excluding Puerto Rico and the Virgin Islands.

Table V. This table summarizes for each of the next three five-year periods the estimated total capital inflow required by regions of the world and the estimated division of these totals between capital aid and private investment. Some elements of what has come to be called "foreign aid" in the American aid program are omitted from these figures (e.g., technical assistance and the emergency fund) because they do not constitute capital inflow in the usual sense. Also excluded are those elements of defense support which do not contribute directly to capital formation; that portion of surplus agricultural products which cannot properly be regarded as providing capital; and expenditures for so-called social development, encompassing such items as education, health, and administration, which are not normally included in economists' statistical estimates of new productive capital.

The first column in this table estimates the capital inflow which would be required to produce the rates of growth assumed as reasonable in Table IV. In general, the method was to estimate total investment requirements by applying a capital-output ratio to the growth figures and then to subtract estimates of the level of domestic savings which each of the countries could be expected to achieve. India bulks so large in the figures for Asia that it has seemed useful to present an alternative estimate for that continent. The first estimate accepts the assumptions made in the draft outline of the Indian Third Five Year Plan as to rates of growth and as to domestic average and marginal savings rates. The alternate estimate is based on somewhat less optimistic assumptions both as to the capital-output ratio and as to domestic savings. The division of capital inflow in the last two columns into capital aid and private investment is based on exceedingly rough estimates and serves only illustrative purposes. In comparing the three periods, it will be noted that the required capital inflow falls off in 1971-1976 because domestic savings are assumed to take over a larger share of the substantially increased capital requirements. It will also be noted that the role of private investment is assumed to increase over the fifteen years.

Table VI

A PROPOSAL FOR SHARING THE BURDEN OF CAPITAL AID*

Country	Number of Families (Thousands) (1)	A. "Money" GNP				Weight Used (6)	B. "Real" GNP			
		GNP per Family (Dollars) (2)	Tax per Family (Dollars) (3)	Contribution (Per Cent)			GNP per Family (Dollars) (7)	Tax per Family (Dollars) (8)	Contribution (Per Cent)	
				With Soviet Union (4)	Without Soviet Union (5)				With Soviet Union (9)	Without Soviet Union (10)
Belgium	2,303.2	5,392	495	1.0	1.1	1.23	6,632	729	1.2	1.4
Canada	4,578.2	7,954	1,002	4.1	4.3	1.00	7,954	1,002	3.4	3.7
Denmark	1,152.7	4,774	380	0.4	0.4	1.33	6,349	676	0.6	0.6
Finland	1,128.5	3,573	164	0.2	0.2	1.44	5,145	449	0.4	0.4
France	11,478.0	4,815	389	4.0	4.2	1.20	5,778	568	4.8	5.3
West Germany	14,470.0	4,452	326	4.1	4.3	1.43	6,366	679	7.0	7.7
Italy	12,385.7	2,491	0	0	0	1.44	3,587	164	1.5	1.6
Luxembourg	83.0	6,084	626	0.04	0.04	1.23	7,483	900	0.05	0.06
Netherlands	2,910.5	3,815	209	0.5	0.6	1.55	5,913	594	1.3	1.4
Norway	906.7	4,895	398	0.3	0.3	1.29	6,315	670	0.4	0.5
Oceania	4,023.7	4,419	317	1.1	1.2	1.33	5,877	585	1.7	1.9
Soviet Union	53,742.0	3,274	110	5.3	—	1.20	3,928	227	9.0	—
Sweden	1,889.7	6,228	653	1.1	1.2	1.30	8,096	1,033	1.4	1.6
Switzerland	1,343.5	6,222	652	0.8	0.8	1.25	7,778	944	0.9	1.0
United Kingdom	13,075.0	5,383	493	5.8	6.1	1.30	6,998	799	7.7	8.4
United States	46,141.5	11,161	1,728	71.3	75.2	1.00	11,161	1,728	58.6	64.4

*Based on the current U.S. progressive income tax schedule. Also assuming GNP per family as a measure of income, with family consisting of four members.

Table VI. This table illustrates the application of a suggested principle for dividing equitably among the developed countries the burden of supplying capital aid to the underdeveloped countries. The principle proposed is that relative shares should be determined by applying to the per family GNP (in dollars) of the developed countries a rate of taxation which progresses with increasing income on the same basis as the present U.S. income tax. In Section A of the table this principle is applied to family incomes expressed in "nominal" or "money" figures, that is, in local currencies converted at the effective rates of exchange. Section B of the table applies the same principle to per family GNP computed in "real" terms, that is, by valuing all elements of GNP at U.S. prices.

SELECTED BIBLIOGRAPHY

Agarwala, A. N., and S. P. Singh, eds. *The Economics of Underdevelopment*. Bombay, New York: Oxford University Press, Indian Branch, 1958.

Allen, Robert L. *Middle Eastern Economic Relations with the Soviet Union, Eastern Europe, and Mainland China*. Charlottesville: University of Virginia Press, 1958.

——. *Soviet Influence in Latin America: The Role of Economic Relations*. Washington: Public Affairs Press, 1959.

Almond, Gabriel A., and James S. Coleman, eds. *The Politics of the Developing Areas*. Princeton: Princeton University Press, 1960.

American Assembly. *International Stability and Progress: United States Interests and Instruments*. New York: Graduate School of Business, Columbia University, 1957.

——. *The United States and Africa*. New York: Graduate School of Business, Columbia University, 1958.

——. *The United States and the Far East*. New York: Graduate School of Business, Columbia University, 1956.

American Academy of Political and Social Science. *Agrarian Societies in Transition*. Edited by Bert F. Hoselitz. (*The Annals,* Vol. 305, May 1956.)

——. *International Co-operation for Social Welfare—A New Reality*. Edited by Hertha Kraus. (*The Annals,* Vol. 329, May 1960.)

——. *Partnership for Progress: International Technical Co-operation*. Edited by Richard W. Gable. (*The Annals,* Vol. 323, May 1959.)

American Economic Association. *Papers and Proceedings. American Economic Review,* Vol. 49, May 1959. See "Fundamentals of Economic Progress in Underdeveloped Countries," pp. 134-178; "Special Problems Facing Underdeveloped Countries," pp. 179-202; "The Role and Character of Foreign Aid," pp. 203-250.

Bailey, F. G. *Caste and the Economic Frontier: A Village in Highland Orissa.* Manchester: Manchester University Press, 1958.

Banfield, Edward C. *The Moral Basis of a Backward Society.* Glencoe, Ill.: Free Press, 1958.

Baran, Paul A. *The Political Economy of Growth.* New York: Monthly Review Press, 1957.

Bascom, William R., and Melville J. Herskovits, eds. *Continuity and Change in African Cultures.* Chicago: University of Chicago Press, 1958.

Bauer, P. T., and Basil S. Yamey. *The Economics of Under-Developed Countries.* Chicago: University of Chicago Press; Cambridge: Cambridge University Press, 1957.

Belshaw, Horace. *Population Growth and Levels of Consumption, with Special Reference to Countries in Asia.* New York: Institute of Pacific Relations, 1956.

Berliner, Joseph S. *Soviet Economic Aid.* New York: Praeger, 1958.

Bonné, Alfred. *Studies in Economic Development with Special Reference to Conditions in the Underdeveloped Areas of Western Asia and India.* London: Routledge, 1957; New York: Humanities Press, 1958.

Bowles, Chester. *Africa's Challenge to America.* Berkeley: University of California Press, 1956.

Brzezinski, Zbigniew. "Politics of Underdevelopment." *World Politics,* Vol. 9, October 1956, pp. 55-75.

Buchanan, Norman S., and Howard S. Ellis. *Approaches to Economic Development.* New York: Twentieth Century Fund, 1955.

Carter, Gwendolen M., and William O. Brown, eds. *Transition in Africa: Studies in Political Adaptation.* Boston: African Research and Studies Program, Boston University, 1958.

Center for International Studies, Massachusetts Institute of Technology. *The Objectives of United States Economic Assistance Programs.* Study prepared for the Committee on Foreign Relations, United States Senate. Washington: Government Printing Office, 1956.

Cleveland, Harlan, Gerard J. Mangone, and John Clarke Adams. *The Overseas Americans.* New York: McGraw-Hill, 1960.

Coale, Ansley J., and Edgar M. Hoover. *Population Growth and Economic Development in Low-Income Countries: A Case Study of India's Prospects.* Princeton: Princeton University Press, 1958.

Coleman, James S. *Nigeria: Background to Nationalism.* Berkeley: University of California Press, 1958.

Dean, Vera Micheles. *The Nature of the Non-Western World.* New York: New American Library, 1957.

Domar, Evsey D. *Essays in the Theory of Economic Growth.* New York: Oxford University Press, 1957.

Dood, Leonard W. *Becoming More Civilized: A Psychological Explanation.* New Haven: Yale University Press, 1960.

Du Bois, Cora A. *Social Forces in Southeast Asia.* Cambridge: Harvard University Press, 1959.

Emerson, Rupert. *From Empire to Nation: The Rise to Self-Assertion of Asian and African Peoples.* Cambridge: Harvard University Press, 1960.

Foreign Policy Clearing House. *Strategy for the 60's.* Summary and Analysis of Studies Prepared by 13 Foreign Policy Research Centers for the United States Senate. Washington, 1961.

Ghose, Subratesh. *Trade Unionism in the Underdeveloped Countries.* Calcutta: Bookland, 1960.

Ginsburg, Norton, ed. *Essays on Geography and Economic Development.* Chicago: University of Chicago Press, 1960.

Gluckman, Max. *Custom and Conflict in Africa.* Oxford: Blackwell, 1959.

Gourou, Pierre. *The Tropical World, Its Social and Economic Conditions and Its Future Status.* Translated by E. D. Laborde. 2nd ed. London, New York: Longmans, Green, 1958.

Hagen, Everett E. "How Economic Growth Begins." *Public Opinion Quarterly,* Vol. 22, Fall 1958, pp. 373-390.

Hance, William A. *African Economic Development.* New York: Harper, 1958.

Hauser, Philip M., ed. *Population and World Politics.* Glencoe, Ill.: Free Press, 1958.

Higgins, Benjamin. *Economic Development: Principles, Problems, and Policies.* New York: Norton, 1959.

Hirschman, Albert O. *The Strategy of Economic Development.* New Haven: Yale University Press, 1958.

Hoselitz, Bert F., ed. *The Progress of Underdeveloped Areas.* Chicago: University of Chicago Press, 1952.

Hoselitz, Bert F., ed. *Sociological Aspects of Economic Development.* Glencoe, Ill.: Free Press, 1960.

International African Institute. *Social Implications of Industrialization and Urbanization in Africa South of the Sahara.* Paris: UNESCO, 1956.

Jackson, Sir Robert. *The Case for an International Development Authority.* Syracuse: Syracuse University Press, 1959.

Jennings, Sir William I. *The Approach to Self-Government.* Cambridge: Cambridge University Press, 1956.

Kahin, George McT., ed. *Government and Politics of Southeast Asia.* Ithaca: Cornell University Press, 1959.

Kerr, Clark, John T. Dunlop, Frederick H. Harbison, and Charles A. Myers. *Industrialism and Industrial Man.* Cambridge: Harvard University Press, 1960.

Kindleberger, Charles P. *Economic Development.* New York: McGraw-Hill, 1958.

Kuznets, Simon. *Six Lectures on Economic Growth.* Glencoe, Ill.: Free Press, 1959.

———, Wilbert E. Moore, and Joseph J. Spengler, eds. *Economic Growth: Brazil, India, Japan.* Durham: Duke University Press, 1955.

Laqueur, Walter Z., ed. *The Middle East in Transition: Studies in Contemporary History.* New York: Praeger, 1958.

Lee, Douglas H. K. *Climate and Economic Development in the Tropics.* New York: Harper, 1957.

Leibenstein, Harvey. *Economic Backwardness and Economic Growth: Studies in the Theory of Economic Development.* New York: Wiley, 1957.

Lerner, Daniel, ed. *Attitude Research in Modernizing Areas.* (*Public Opinion Quarterly,* Vol. 22, Fall 1958, pp. 217-420.)

———. *The Passing of Traditional Society: Modernizing the Middle East.* Glencoe, Ill.: Free Press, 1958.

Lewis, W. Arthur. *The Theory of Economic Growth.* Homewood, Ill.: Irwin, 1955.

Lipset, Seymour M. "Some Social Requisites of Democracy: Economic Development and Political Legitimacy." *American Political Science Review,* Vol. 53, March 1959.

Liska, George. *The New Statecraft: Foreign Aid in American Foreign Policy.* Chicago: University of Chicago Press, 1960.

Makal, Mahmut. *A Village in Anatolia.* Translated from the Turkish by Sir Wyndham Deeds. London: Vallentine, Mitchell, 1954.

Mannoni, O. *Prospero and Caliban: The Psychology of Colonization.* Translated by Pamela Powesland. New York: Praeger, 1956.

Mason, Edward S. *Economic Planning in Underdeveloped Areas: Government and Business.* New York: Fordham University Press, 1958.

Mead, Margaret, ed. *Cultural Patterns and Technical Change.* Paris: UNESCO, 1953; New York: Mentor, 1955.

———. *New Lives for Old.* New York: Morrow, 1956.

Meier, Gerald M., and Robert E. Baldwin. *Economic Development: Theory, History, Policy.* New York: Wiley, 1957.

Meyer, A. J. *Middle Eastern Capitalism: Nine Essays.* Cambridge: Harvard University Press, 1959.

Millikan, Max F., ed. *Investment Criteria and Economic Growth.* Cambridge: Center for International Studies, Massachusetts Institute of Technology, 1955; Bombay: Asia Publishing House, 1961.

———, and W. W. Rostow. *A Proposal: Key to an Effective Foreign Policy.* New York: Harper, 1957.

Moore, Wilbert E. *Industrialization and Labor: Social Aspects of Economic Development.* Ithaca: Cornell University Press, 1951.

Myrdal, Gunnar. *Beyond the Welfare State: Economic Planning and Its International Implications.* New Haven: Yale University Press, 1960.

———. *Rich Lands and Poor: The Road to World Prosperity.* New York: Harper, 1958.

National Bureau of Economic Research. *Capital Formation and Economic Growth.* Princeton: Princeton University Press, 1955.

National Planning Association. Reports on *The Economics of Competitive Coexistence.* Washington, 1959.

Norman, E. Herbert. *Japan's Emergence as a Modern State.* New York: Institute of Pacific Relations, 1940.

Nurkse, Ragnar. *Problems of Capital Formation in Underdeveloped Countries.* 3rd ed. Oxford: Blackwell, 1955.

Panikkar, K. M. *The Afro-Asian States and Their Problems.* New York: Day, 1959.

Papanek, Gustav F. "Framing a Development Program." *International Conciliation,* No. 527, March 1960, pp. 307-372.

Park, Richard L., and Irene Tinker, eds. *Leadership and Political Institutions in India.* Princeton: Princeton University Press, 1959.

Pool, Ithiel de Sola, ed. *Public Opinion Quarterly,* Vol. 20, Spring 1956. See "Communication and Politics in Pre-Industrial Regions," pp. 249-298.

Pye, Lucian W. "The Non-Western Political Process." *Journal of Politics,* Vol. 20, August 1958, pp. 468-486.

Read, Margaret. *Education and Social Change in Tropical Areas.* London, New York: Nelson, 1955.

Redfield, Robert. *Peasant Society and Culture: An Anthropological Approach to Civilization.* Chicago: University of Chicago Press, 1956.

Rivkin, Arnold. *Africa and the West: Elements of Free World Policy.* New York: Praeger, 1961.

Rockefeller Brothers Fund. *Foreign Economic Policy for the Twentieth Century.* New York: Doubleday, 1958.

Rostow, W. W. *The Process of Economic Growth.* New York: Norton, 1952.

———. *The Stages of Economic Growth: A Non-Communist Manifesto.* Cambridge: Cambridge University Press, 1960.

———. "The Take-Off into Self-Sustained Growth." *The Economic Journal,* Vol. 66, March 1956, pp. 25-48.

Shannon, Lyle W. "Is the Level of Development Related to Capacity for Self-Government?" *American Journal of Economics and Sociology,* Vol. 17, July 1958.

———. "Socio-Economic Development and Political Status." *Social Problems,* Vol. 7, Fall 1959, pp. 157-169.

———. *Underdeveloped Areas: A Book of Readings and Research.* New York: Harper, 1957.

Shils, Edward B. "The Concentration and Dispersion of Charisma: Their Bearing on Economic Policy in Underdeveloped Countries." *World Politics,* Vol. 11, October 1958, pp. 1-19.

———. "Intellectuals, Public Opinion, and Economic Development." *World Politics,* Vol. 10, January 1958, pp. 232-255.

Smelser, Neil J. *Social Change in the Industrial Revolution: An Application of Theory to the British Cotton Industry.* Chicago: University of Chicago Press, 1959.

Smith, Prudence, ed. *Africa in Transition.* London: Reinhardt, 1958.

Smith, Thomas C. *The Agrarian Origins of Modern Japan.* Stanford: Stanford University Press, 1959.

———. *Political Change and Industrial Development in Japan: Government Enterprise, 1868-1880.* Stanford: Stanford University Press, 1955.

Spengler, Joseph J., and O. D. Duncan. *Population Theory and Policy.* Glencoe, Ill.: Free Press, 1956.

Spicer, Edward Holland. *Human Problems in Technological Change: A Casebook.* New York: Russell Sage Foundation, 1952.

Staley, Eugene. *The Future of Underdeveloped Countries: Political Implications of Economic Development.* New York: Harper, 1954.

Thayer, Philip, ed. *Tensions in the Middle East.* Baltimore: Johns Hopkins Press, 1958.

Tinbergen, Jan. *The Design of Development.* Baltimore: Johns Hopkins Press, 1958.

United Nations. Department of Economic Affairs. *Measures for the Economic Development of Under-Developed Countries.* New York, May 1951.

United States. President's Committee to Study the United States Military Assistance Program. *Composite Report.* Washington: Government Printing Office, August 1959. 2 vols. (Draper Report.)

Useem, John, and Ruth Hill. *The Western-Educated Man in India: A Study of His Social Roles and Influence.* New York: Dryden, 1955.

Vakil, C. N., and P. R. Brahmanand. *Planning for an Expanding Economy: Accumulation, Employment, and Technical Progress in Underdeveloped Countries.* Bombay: Vora, 1956.

Viner, Jacob. *International Trade and Economic Development.* Glencoe, Ill.: Free Press, 1952.

Warriner, Doreen. *Land Reform and Development in the Middle East: A Study of Egypt, Syria, and Iraq.* London: Royal Institute of International Affairs, 1957.

Weiner, Myron. *Party Politics in India: The Development of a Multi-Party System.* Princeton: Princeton University Press, 1957.

Wolf, Charles, Jr. *Foreign Aid: Theory and Practice in Southern Asia.* Princeton: Princeton University Press, 1960.

———, and Sidney C. Sufrin. *Capital Formation and Foreign Investment in Underdeveloped Areas.* Syracuse: Syracuse University Press, 1955.

Zinkin, Maurice. *Development for Free Asia.* Fair Lawn, N.J.: Essential; London: Chatto & Windus, 1956.

Useful Bibliographies

American Universities Field Staff, Inc. *A Select Bibliography: Asia, Africa, Eastern Europe, Latin America.* New York, 1960.

Hald, Marjorie. *Selected Bibliography on Economic Development and Foreign Aid.* Santa Monica: RAND, 1957.

Hazlewood, Arthur, comp. *The Economics of 'Under-Developed' Areas: An Annotated Reading List of Books, Articles, and Official Publications.* 2nd ed. London: Oxford University Press, 1959.

Princeton University. Industrial Relations Section. *Manpower Problems in Economic Development: A Selected Bibliography.* Princeton, 1958.

BOOKS FROM THE CENTER
FOR INTERNATIONAL STUDIES

AN AMERICAN POLICY IN ASIA, W. W. Rostow and Richard W. Hatch, Technology Press and Wiley, 1955

THE AMERICAN STYLE: *Essays in Value and Performance,* Elting E. Morison, ed., Harper, 1958

BLOC POLITICS IN THE UNITED NATIONS, Thomas Hovet, Jr., Harvard, 1960

CHANGING IMAGES OF AMERICA: *A Study of Indian Students' Perceptions,* George V. Coelho, Free Press, 1958

THE CHINESE FAMILY IN THE COMMUNIST REVOLUTION, C. K. Yang, Technology Press, 1959

A CHINESE VILLAGE IN EARLY COMMUNIST TRANSITION, C. K. Yang, Technology Press, 1959

COERCIVE PERSUASION: *A Socio-Psychological Analysis of the Brainwashing of American Civilians by the Chinese Communists,* Edgar H. Schein in collaboration with Inge Schneier and Curtis Barker, Norton, 1961

EAST AND WEST IN INDIA'S DEVELOPMENT, Wilfred Malenbaum, National Planning Association, 1959

THE ECONOMIC DEVELOPMENT OF BURMA, Everett E. Hagen, National Planning Association, 1956

THE ECONOMICS OF COMMUNIST EASTERN EUROPE, Nicolas Spulber, Technology Press and Wiley, 1957

FINANCING ECONOMIC DEVELOPMENT: *The Indonesian Case,* Douglas S. Paauw, Free Press, 1960

HANDBOOK FOR INDUSTRY STUDIES, Everett E. Hagen, Free Press, 1958

INDONESIA'S ECONOMIC STABILIZATION AND DEVELOPMENT, Benjamin Higgins, Institute of Pacific Relations, 1957

INDUSTRIAL CHANGE IN INDIA: *Industrial Growth, Capital Requirements, and Technological Change, 1937-1955,* George Rosen, Free Press, 1958

INDUSTRIAL GROWTH IN SOUTH INDIA: *Case Studies in Economic Development,* George B. Baldwin, Free Press, 1959

THE JAPANESE FACTORY: *Aspects of Its Social Organization,* James C. Abegglen, Free Press, 1958

JAPANESE POPULAR CULTURE: *Studies in Mass Communication and Cultural Change,* Hidetoshi Kato, ed. and trans., Tuttle, 1959

NUCLEAR POWER AND ITALY'S ENERGY POSITION, P. N. Rosenstein-Rodan and I. M. D. Little, National Planning Association, 1957

OVERSEAS CHINESE NATIONALISM: *The Genesis of the Pan-Chinese Movement in Indonesia, 1900-1916,* Lea E. Williams, Free Press, 1960

THE PASSING OF TRADITIONAL SOCIETY: *Modernizing the Middle East,* Daniel Lerner, with Lucille W. Pevsner, Free Press, 1958

POSTWAR ECONOMIC TRENDS IN THE UNITED STATES, Ralph E. Freeman, ed., Harper, 1960

A PROPOSAL: *Key to an Effective Foreign Policy,* Max F. Millikan and W. W. Rostow, Harper, 1957

THE PROSPECTS FOR COMMUNIST CHINA, W. W. Rostow and others, Technology Press and Wiley, 1954

THE QUESTION OF GOVERNMENT SPENDING: *Public Needs and Private Wants,* Francis M. Bator, Harper, 1960

THE RELIGION OF JAVA, Clifford Geertz, Free Press, 1960

SCRATCHES ON OUR MINDS: *American Images of China and India,* Harold R. Isaacs, John Day, 1958

SOME ASPECTS OF INDUSTRIAL FINANCE IN INDIA, George Rosen, Asia, 1961

SOVIET EDUCATION FOR SCIENCE AND TECHNOLOGY, Alexander G. Korol, Technology Press and Wiley, 1957

THE STRUCTURE OF THE EAST GERMAN ECONOMY, Wolfgang F. Stolper, with Karl W. Roskamp, Harvard, 1960

THE UNITED NATIONS AND U.S. FOREIGN POLICY: *A New Look at the National Interest,* Lincoln P. Bloomfield, Little, Brown, 1960

THE UNITED STATES IN THE WORLD ARENA, W. W. Rostow, Harper, 1960

171